Holiday FOOD FUN

Creative Ideas for Halloween, Thanksgiving, Christmas & More

BEFORE YOU BEGIN

Make your holidays even more special with these delightful ideas for unique decorations, place cards, party favors and gifts, all created in your kitchen. Every one of these fabulous projects has easy-to-follow, step-by-step directions, and many are beautifully photographed. Read through the following information before starting. You will discover many helpful tips and important guidelines to make your holiday preparations easier and more fun!

GENERAL GUIDELINES

- Read the entire recipe before beginning to make sure you have all the necessary ingredients, utensils and supplies.

- Measure all the ingredients accurately and assemble them in the order called for in the recipe.

- Prepare pans and baking sheets according to the recipe directions.

- Follow the recipe directions and baking times exactly. Check for doneness using the test given in the recipe.

- Before serving any of the beautiful projects you've created, be sure to remove any inedible decorations or wooden toothpicks.

SUPPLIES

Some of the projects in *Holiday Food Fun* call for special equipment or other nonfood items; these are always listed in the recipe under the heading SUPPLIES. Using the supplies makes the project easier and also gives the final product a more professional look. Most of the supplies listed are available in stores carrying cake decorating equipment and in supermarkets. Other supplies may be found around the house or at craft stores.

Kitchen Equipment

Some special baking pans are listed under SUPPLIES. Other pans and equipment normally found in a well-equipped kitchen are not listed. The equipment *not* listed includes: mixing bowls, baking and cookie sheets, 13 × 9-inch pan, 8 × 8-inch pan, 8-inch round pan, 9-inch springform pan, 9-inch pie plate, 5-cup ring mold and small, medium and large saucepans.

2

Additional equipment you may need that is listed under SUPPLIES includes: pastry brush, paper and foil baking cups, parchment paper, craft sticks, lollipop sticks, cookie cutters and a candy/deep-fry thermometer. See the following explanations for details on other essential supplies such as cake boards and pastry bags with decorating tips.

Cake Boards

Some of the projects in this book are too large for standard serving plates and platters. Cake boards, cutting boards, cookie sheets or other large flat surfaces can be used instead. Cake boards are made from heavy cardboard and can be covered with foil, greaseproof paper or plastic wrap. To cover, cut the foil or paper 1 to 2 inches larger than the board. Center the board on the reverse side of the paper. Cut slashes in the paper almost to the board along any place that is curved. This allows the paper to fit smoothly over the board. Fold the edges over the board and tape into place. If an item is very large or heavy, two cake boards may be stacked together before covering for additional support.

Pastry Bags and Decorating Tips

A pastry bag with several tips is essential for piping decorations. The pastry bag can be a plastic disposable bag, a reusable bag or a bag folded from a parchment paper triangle. Some

basic decorating tips that are called for in the recipes are small, medium and large writing tips and medium and large star tips.

Paste Food Color

Although not absolutely necessary, paste food color can give better results by producing bright, vibrant hues and it does not thin the mixture like liquid color. To color, add a *small* amount of paste food color with a wooden toothpick to the mixture and stir well. Slowly add more color until the desired shade is reached.

SPECIAL TECHNIQUES

Making Patterns

When a pattern is to be used only once, as for the Jolly Ole Saint Nick Cake, make the pattern out of waxed paper. Using the diagram(s) and photo as guides, draw the pattern pieces on waxed paper. Cut the pieces out and place them on the cake. Cut around the pattern pieces with a sharp knife. Remove the pattern pieces and discard. Continue as directed in the recipe.

For patterns that are used more than once, as when making cookies, make the pattern more durable by using clean lightweight cardboard or poster board. Using the diagram(s) and photo as guides, draw the pattern pieces on the cardboard. Cut the pieces out and lightly spray one side with cooking spray. Place the pattern pieces on the rolled out dough or pastry, sprayed side down, and cut around them with a sharp knife. Reuse the pattern pieces to make as many cutouts as needed.

Frosting

In many of the projects commercially prepared frosting is called for, however, you may use your own favorite frosting recipe if you wish. When using frosting for piping and other decorations, the proper consistency is essential for success. The frosting should hold its shape when scooped with a spatula. If it is too soft, try refrigerating the frosting first and keep it chilled while working.

Piping Frosting

To fill a pastry bag with frosting, insert the decorating tip first. Fold the top of the bag down to form a cuff and use a spatula to fill the bag about half full. Unfold the top of the bag and twist it down tightly against the frosting.

Grip the pastry bag near the top with the twisted end between your thumb and forefinger. Place your other hand near the tip. Using even pressure, squeeze the frosting out while guiding the tip. Do not loosen your grip on the twisted end or the frosting will begin to push up and out of the top of the bag.

Different decorating tips produce different piped decorations. Writing tips have round holes and make smooth lines perfect for lettering and outlining. A star tip makes individual stars or fancy ridged stripes and zigzags. With a little practice, there is no end to the variety of piped decorations you can make.

For simple piped decorations a reclosable plastic sandwich bag works great as a substitute for a pastry bag fitted with a writing tip. Fold the top of the bag down to form a cuff and use a spatula to fill the bag about half full with frosting. Unfold the top of the bag and twist it down tightly against the frosting. Snip a tiny tip (about $\frac{1}{8}$ inch) off one corner of the bag. Hold the top of the bag tightly and squeeze the frosting through the opening. The more you cut off the corner of the bag, the wider the piping will be.

Melting Chocolate

When melting chocolate be sure the utensils are completely dry. Any drop of moisture makes the chocolate become stiff and grainy. If this does happen, add $\frac{1}{2}$ teaspoon shortening (not butter) for each ounce of chocolate and stir until smooth. Chocolate scorches easily, and once scorched cannot be used. Chocolate will melt more evenly when coarsely chopped. Follow one of the following three methods for successful melting.

Double Boiler: Place the chocolate in the top of a double boiler or in a heatproof bowl over hot, not boiling water. Stir until smooth. (Make sure the water remains just below a simmer and is 1 inch below the top pan.) Be careful that no steam or water gets into the chocolate.

Direct Heat: Place the chocolate in a heavy saucepan and melt over very low heat, stirring constantly. Remove the chocolate from the heat as soon as it is melted. Be sure to watch the chocolate carefully since it is easily scorched with this method.

Microwave Oven: Place a 1-ounce square or 1 cup chocolate chips in a small microwavable bowl. Microwave on HIGH 1 to 2 minutes or until the chocolate is almost melted, stirring well after every minute. Add 10 seconds for each additional ounce of chocolate. Be sure to stir the microwaved chocolate well because it retains its original shape even when melted.

Piping Chocolate

If you'll be piping melted chocolate, use this easy one-step method. Place about ½ cup chocolate chips or a 1-ounce square of chocolate in a reclosable plastic sandwich bag. Close bag tightly. Microwave on HIGH about 1 minute; knead chocolate until it's melted. Repeat if necessary, microwaving 30 seconds at a time. Twist the top of the bag tightly against the chocolate. Snip a tiny tip (about ⅛ inch) off one corner of the bag. Hold the top of the bag tightly and pipe the chocolate through the opening. This method is great for piping the numbers and clock hands for the Minutes to Midnight Cake or for adding a chocolate drizzle to a cake or cookies.

Tinting Coconut

Dilute a few drops of food color with ½ teaspoon water in a large plastic bag. Add 1 to 1⅓ cups flaked coconut. Close the bag and shake well until the coconut is evenly coated. If a deeper color is desired, add more diluted food color and shake again.

HAVE FUN

Page through each chapter to see all the wonderful ways to set the mood for your next celebration. Choose a number of ideas to adorn your holiday table or set aside a day to do projects with the whole family. Don't get locked into the suggestions given in the recipes and photos. Feel free to change the colors, shapes or decorations to suit your party. Let your imagination and creativity take over and have a great time making a holiday masterpiece or maybe starting a new family tradition.

HALLOWEEN

Halloween Haunted House

Empty milk cartons are the secret to making this rickety house a spooky success. Let your guests devour the windows, doors and even the resident ghost—if they dare!

INGREDIENTS

- **1 container (16 ounces) chocolate fudge frosting**
  Decorations: Pretzel sticks, nuts, fudge-coated graham crackers, black licorice twists, black jelly beans, sugar wafers, candy corn, dried papaya, rice crackers, and other assorted candies
- **1 Spooky Ghost Cookie (page 27), optional**

SUPPLIES

- **2 empty 1-quart milk cartons, rinsed and dried**
- **1 (13 × 11-inch) cake board, covered, or large tray**

1. Tape each milk carton closed at top. Tape milk cartons together to make house; wrap with foil. Attach securely to covered cake board with tape.

2. Frost cartons with chocolate frosting; decorate as shown in photo using frosting to attach decorations. Attach Spooky Ghost Cookie with frosting, if desired.   *Makes 1 house*

Halloween Haunted House

The Great Pumpkin Cookie

Use this huge cookie as a colorful party centerpiece. Then break or cut into pieces and serve for dessert.

INGREDIENTS

- **1 recipe Butter Cookie dough (page 93)**
- **1 container (16 ounces) vanilla frosting**
  Assorted food colors

SUPPLIES

- **Pastry bag and medium writing tip**

1. Preheat oven to 350°F. Line 12-inch pizza pan with foil. Press cookie dough evenly into prepared pan.

2. Bake 15 to 20 minutes until edges just begin to brown. Cool completely in pan on wire rack. Remove from pan; peel off foil.

3. Color ½ of frosting orange. Frost cookie. Color remaining frosting as desired. Using pastry bag fitted with medium writing tip, pipe jack-o'-lantern face on cookie.   *Makes 1 large cookie (about 12 servings)*

Clockwise from top left: *Witches' Brew; Trick-or-Treat Caramel Apples (page 12); Friendly Ghost Puffs*

Witches' Brew

There's no "eye of newt" in this brew — just a chocolately good cinnamon flavor and witches' broomstick stirrers.

**Witches' Broomsticks
    (recipe follows)**
½ **cup water**
¼ **cup red cinnamon
    candies**
 6 **cups milk**
½ **cup chocolate drink mix**

1. Prepare Witches' Broomsticks; set aside.

2. Bring water and cinnamon candies to a boil over medium-high heat in medium saucepan, stirring until candies melt. Add milk; whisk in drink mix. Bring to a simmer over medium-high heat.

3. Pour into mugs. Serve warm with Witches' Broomsticks as stirrers.   *Makes 8 servings (about 6 ounces each)*

8

Witches' Broomsticks

**8 gumdrop orange slices
8 cinnamon sticks (each
about 5 inches long)
2 black licorice whips**

1. Roll gumdrop orange slices into triangles with rolling pin on surface lightly sprinkled with sugar. With wet scissors, snip bottom of triangles for broom bristles.

2. For each broomstick, wrap narrow end of triangle around cinnamon stick to make broom bristles. Tie in place with short piece of licorice whip.

Makes 8 broomsticks

Friendly Ghost Puffs

These puffs can easily be made in advance and filled just before serving. Just wrap the unfilled puffs tightly in foil or plastic wrap and store in a cool place for up to 2 days.

**1 cup water
½ cup butter or margarine,
cut into pieces
1 cup all-purpose flour
¼ teaspoon salt
4 eggs
1 quart orange sherbet
Confectioners' sugar
16 chocolate chips**

1. Bring water and butter to a boil in medium saucepan over high heat, stirring until butter is melted. Reduce heat to low; stir in flour and salt until mixture forms a ball. Remove from heat.

Add eggs, one at a time, beating after each addition until mixture is smooth.

2. Preheat oven to 400°F. Spoon about ⅓ cup dough onto ungreased baking sheet. With wet knife, form into ghost shape as shown in diagram. Repeat with remaining dough to form ghosts, spacing them about 2 inches apart.

3. Bake 40 to 45 minutes or until puffed and golden. Remove to wire racks; cool completely.

4. Carefully cut each ghost in half horizontally; remove soft interior leaving hollow shell.

5. Just before serving, fill each shell bottom with about ½ cup orange sherbet. Cover with top of shell; sprinkle with confectioners' sugar. Position 2 chocolate chips on each ghost for eyes. *Makes 8 ghosts*

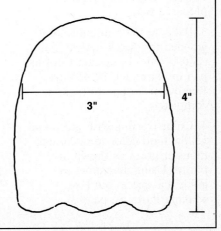

Macho Monster Cake

What fun to decorate a cake that is supposed to look ugly! Make your monster as scary as you can.

INGREDIENTS

1 package (18.25 ounces) cake mix, any flavor, plus ingredients to prepare mix
1 container (16 ounces) cream cheese or vanilla frosting
Green and yellow food color
Black decorating gel
1 white chocolate baking bar (2 ounces)

SUPPLIES

1 (13 × 9-inch) cake board, covered, or large tray

1. Preheat oven to 350°F. Grease and flour 13 × 9-inch baking pan.

2. Prepare cake mix according to package directions. Pour into prepared pan.

3. Bake 30 to 35 minutes until wooden toothpick inserted into center comes out clean. Cool in pan on wire rack 10 minutes. Remove from pan to rack; cool completely.

4. Color frosting with green and yellow food color to make ugly monster green as shown in photo. Using diagram 1 as guide, cut pieces out (see Making Patterns, page 3).

5. Position pieces on prepared cake board as shown in diagram 2, connecting with some frosting. Frost cake. Using decorating gel, pipe eyes, mouth, hair and scars as shown. Break white chocolate baking bar into irregular pieces; position inside mouth as teeth.

Makes 12 servings

Note: For cleaner cutting lines and fewer crumbs, place the cooled cake in the freezer for 30 to 45 minutes before cutting.

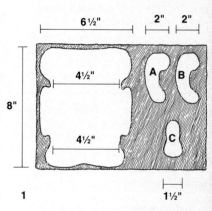

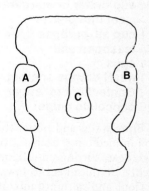

Macho Monster Cake

Trick-or-Treat Caramel Apples

Older children can help make these easy, fun-looking Halloween apples.

INGREDIENTS
  **1 package (14 ounces)
    chocolate caramels,*
    unwrapped
  1 cup miniature
    marshmallows
  1 tablespoon water
  5 or 6 medium apples
    Decorations: Candy corn,
    red cinnamon candies,
    jelly beans, licorice
    whips, candy-coated
    licorice, licorice drops
    and colored sprinkles**

SUPPLIES
  **5 or 6 (2½-inch) paper baking
    cups
  5 or 6 wooden craft sticks**

*Can be made with any flavor caramels.

1. Place paper baking cups on baking sheet. Flatten cups.

2. Combine caramels, marshmallows and water in medium saucepan. Cook over medium heat, stirring constantly, until caramels melt.

3. Rinse and thoroughly dry apples. Insert wooden sticks into stem ends.

4. Dip apple into caramel mixture, coating thoroughly. Remove excess caramel mixture by scraping apple bottom across rim of saucepan. Place on baking cup.

5. Immediately decorate with candies to create face or other design as shown in photo on page 8. (Work quickly or caramel may harden and decorations will not adhere.) Repeat with remaining apples. Refrigerate until firm.

Makes 5 or 6 servings

Pumpkin Patch Place Cards

In addition to guiding your guests where to sit, these cute place cards make yummy take-home treats.

  **8 fudge-coated graham
    crackers
    Green decorating icing
  8 chocolate sandwich
    cookies
  ½ cup chocolate fudge
    frosting
  ½ cup shredded coconut,
    tinted green*
  8 pumpkin candies**

*See Tinting Coconut, page 5.

1. Write names on graham crackers with icing.

2. Attach graham crackers to sandwich cookies at right angles with frosting as shown in photo. Position coconut and pumpkin candies on sandwich cookie as shown, attaching with frosting.

Makes 8 place cards

From left to right: *Pumpkin Patch Place Cards; Funny Bugs Place Cards*

Funny Bugs Place Cards

What fun to have a goofy bug watching you all through dinner.

8 (3-inch) oatmeal cookies
½ cup Fluffy White Frosting (page 93)
16 miniature chocolate sandwich cookies
8 red gumdrops
16 cheese corn curls
8 fudge-covered wafer cookies
White decorating icing

1. Frost oatmeal cookies with Fluffy White Frosting. Position sandwich cookies to make eyes as shown in photo. Attach gumdrop mouths and corn curl antennae as shown.

2. Write names on wafer cookies with icing. Attach to oatmeal cookies with frosting.

Makes 8 place cards

13

Sloppy Goblins

Sloppy joes take on a new taste and persona with the addition of hot dogs and frightening goblin faces.

1 pound lean ground beef
1 cup chopped onion
8 ounces hot dogs
   (about 5), cut into
   ½-inch pieces
¼ cup chopped dill pickle
½ cup ketchup
¼ cup honey
¼ cup tomato paste
¼ cup prepared mustard
2 teaspoons cider vinegar
1 teaspoon Worcestershire
   sauce
8 hamburger buns
   Decorations: Green
   olives, ripe olives,
   banana pepper slices,
   carrot curls and
   crinkles, red pepper,
   parsley sprigs and
   pretzel sticks

1. Cook beef and onion in large skillet over medium heat until beef is brown and onion is tender; drain. Stir in remaining ingredients except buns and decorations. Cook, covered, 5 minutes or until heated through.

2. Spoon meat mixture onto bottoms of buns; cover with tops of buns. Serve with decorations and let each person create their own goblin face. Refrigerate leftovers.   *Makes 8 servings*

From top to bottom: *Sloppy Goblins; Devilish Delights*

Devilish Delights

Your guests will be "tempted" to ask for seconds when they taste these devilishly delicious chicken pies.

1 package (16 ounces)
   hot roll mix, plus
   ingredients to prepare
   mix
1 pound boneless skinless
   chicken breasts, cut
   into ¾-inch pieces
2 tablespoons vegetable
   oil, divided
¾ cup chopped onion
1 clove garlic, minced
1¼ cups sliced zucchini
1 can (8 ounces) peeled
   diced tomatoes, drained
1 can (4 ounces) sliced
   mushrooms, drained
1 teaspoon dried basil
   leaves
½ teaspoon dried oregano
   leaves
   Salt and pepper
1 cup (4 ounces) shredded
   mozzarella cheese
1 egg yolk
1 teaspoon water
   Red food color

1. Prepare hot roll mix according to package directions. Knead dough on lightly floured surface until smooth, about 5 minutes. Cover loosely; let stand about 15 minutes.

2. Cook chicken in 1 tablespoon oil in large skillet over medium-high heat 5 to 6 minutes or until
continued

15

Devilish Delights *continued*

no longer pink in center; remove from skillet and set aside. Cook and stir onion and garlic in remaining 1 tablespoon oil in skillet until tender.

3. Stir in zucchini, tomatoes, mushrooms, basil and oregano; bring to a boil. Reduce heat; simmer 5 to 10 minutes or until excess liquid has evaporated. Stir in reserved chicken; cook 1 minute. Remove from heat; season to taste with salt and pepper. Stir in cheese.

4. Preheat oven to 400°F. Grease baking sheets.

5. Roll dough on floured surface to ¼-inch thickness. Cut into equal number of 4-inch circles. Combine scraps and reroll dough if necessary. Place half of circles on prepared baking sheets. Spoon about ¼ cup chicken mixture on half of the circles; top with remaining circles and seal edges with fork. Cut vents to resemble devil and use dough scraps to make horns, eyes, nose and beard as shown in photo on page 14.

6. Combine egg yolk and water; brush dough. Add red food color to remaining egg yolk mixture. Brush horns and beard with colored egg wash.

7. Bake 20 to 25 minutes or until golden. Refrigerate leftovers.

Makes 10 to 12 servings

Jack-O'-Lantern Cheese Ball

A touch of pumpkin and spices lend a delightful flavor to this distinctive cheese ball.

- **2 cups (8 ounces) shredded Cheddar cheese**
- **½ (8-ounce) package cream cheese, softened**
- **¼ cup solid pack pumpkin**
- **¼ cup pineapple preserves**
- **¼ teaspoon ground allspice**
- **¼ teaspoon ground nutmeg**
- **1 pretzel rod, broken in half**
  Decorations: Dark rye bread, red pepper, black olive slices, parsley sprigs
  Assorted crackers

1. Beat cheeses, pumpkin, preserves and spices in medium bowl until smooth. Cover; refrigerate 2 to 3 hours or until cheese is firm enough to shape.

2. Shape mixture into round pumpkin; place on serving plate. Using knife, score vertical lines down pumpkin as shown in photo. Place pretzel rod in top for stem.

3. Cut bread into triangles for eyes as shown. Decorate pumpkin using bread, pepper, olives and parsley as shown.

4. Cover loosely; refrigerate until serving time. Serve with crackers.

Makes 16 to 18 servings

Jack-O'-Lantern Cheese Ball

Sticks 'n' Stones

For make-ahead convenience, prepare up to 1 week in advance and store in an airtight container.

INGREDIENTS

- 4 cups caramel corn
- 4 cups unseasoned croutons
- ¾ cup sesame sticks
- ¾ cup honey roasted peanuts
- ¾ cup toasted pumpkin or sunflower seeds*
- ¼ cup butter, melted
- 1 package (1 ounce) ranch salad dressing mix
- 10 flat-bottomed ice cream cones

SUPPLIES

Black and gold ribbon

*To toast seeds, place in single layer on baking sheet. Bake at 350°F for 7 to 10 minutes or until golden brown, stirring occasionally. Cool completely.

1. Preheat oven to 300°F.

2. Combine caramel corn, croutons, sesame sticks, peanuts and toasted pumpkin seeds on ungreased jelly-roll pan. Drizzle with butter; sprinkle with dressing mix and toss to coat.

3. Bake 15 minutes, stirring occasionally. Cool 10 minutes on pan. Turn out onto paper towels; cool completely.

4. Tie cones with ribbon as shown in photo. Serve snack mix in cones. *Makes 10 cups*

Leapin' Lizards!

Green and gooey, these lizards are as much fun to make as they are to eat.

INGREDIENTS

- 1 cup butterscotch-flavor chips
- ½ cup corn syrup
- 3 tablespoons butter or margarine
- 1 cup vanilla milk chips
  Green food color
- 7 cups crisped rice cereal
  Decorations: Candy corn, green jelly beans, red miniature jaw breakers and chocolate chips

1. Line baking sheet with waxed paper.

2. Combine butterscotch chips, corn syrup and butter in large saucepan. Stir over medium heat until chips are melted. Add vanilla chips and green food color; stir well. Remove from heat. Add cereal; stir to coat evenly.

3. Lightly butter hands and shape about 1½ cups cereal mixture into lizard (about 6 inches long) as shown in photo. Place on prepared baking sheet. Decorate with candies as shown. Repeat with remaining mixture.

Makes 4 lizards

From top right to bottom:
Sticks 'n' Stones; Leapin' Lizards!;
Magic Wands (page 21)

18

Crazy Cat Cake

Crazy Cat Cake

Use your imagination to make this cat look really crazy.

INGREDIENTS

1 package (18.25 ounces) devil's food cake mix, plus ingredients to prepare mix
1 container (16 ounces) chocolate fudge frosting
Decorations: Red and green gumdrops, pretzel sticks, black licorice whips, black jelly beans

SUPPLIES

1 (13 × 11-inch) cake board, covered, or large tray

1. Preheat oven to 350°F. Grease and flour 1-quart ovenproof bowl, 2-cup ovenproof bowl and 5-cup ovenproof ring mold.

2. Prepare cake mix according to package directions. Pour batter into prepared bowls and mold, filling each about half full.

3. Bake until wooden toothpick inserted into centers comes out clean, about 30 minutes for 2-cup bowl and ring mold and 40 minutes for 1-quart bowl. Cool

in bowls/mold on wire racks 10 minutes. Remove cakes to racks; cool completely.

4. Cut ring cake as shown in diagram 1. Position cakes on prepared cake board as shown in diagram 2, connecting with some frosting. Frost cake. Decorate as shown in photo.

Makes 12 servings

Note: *For cleaner cutting lines and fewer crumbs, place the cooled cake in the freezer for 30 to 45 minutes before cutting.*

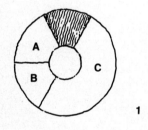

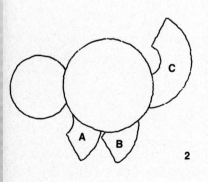

Magic Wands

These magical wands cast a delicious spell over your party.

INGREDIENTS
  1 cup semisweet chocolate chips
  12 pretzel rods
  3 ounces confectionery coating or white chocolate baking bars
  Red and yellow food color
  Assorted sprinkles

SUPPLIES
  Ribbon

1. Line baking sheet with waxed paper.

2. Melt semisweet chocolate in top of double boiler over hot, not boiling, water. Remove from heat. Dip pretzel rods into chocolate, spooning chocolate to coat about ¾ of pretzels. Place on prepared baking sheet. Refrigerate until chocolate is firm.

3. Melt white chocolate in top of double boiler over hot, not boiling water. Stir in food colors to make orange. Remove from heat. Dip coated pretzels quickly into colored chocolate to coat about ¼ of pretzels.

4. Place on baking sheet. Immediately top with sprinkles. Refrigerate until chocolate is firm.

5. Tie ends with ribbons as shown in photo on page 19.

Makes 1 dozen wands

HALLOWEEN

Magic Potion

Kids will love this "magical" punch with its glowing worm-filled ice ring.

Creepy Crawler Ice Ring (recipe follows)
1 cup boiling water
2 packages (4-serving size *each*) lime-flavor gelatin
3 cups cold water
1½ quarts carbonated lemon-lime beverage, chilled
½ cup superfine sugar
Additional gummy worms, optional

1. Prepare Creepy Crawler Ice Ring.

2. Pour boiling water over gelatin in heatproof punch bowl; stir until gelatin dissolves. Stir in cold water. Add lemon-lime beverage and sugar; stir well (mixture will foam for several minutes).

3. Unmold ice ring by dipping bottom of mold briefly into hot water. Float ice ring in punch. Serve cups of punch garnished with gummy worms, if desired.

Makes 10 servings (about 8 ounces each)

Creepy Crawler Ice Ring

1 cup gummy worms or other creepy crawler candy
1 quart lemon-lime thirst quencher beverage

Magic Potion

Arrange gummy worms in bottom of 5-cup ring mold; fill mold with thirst quencher beverage. Freeze until solid, 8 hours or overnight.

Tombstone Brownies

Chocolate bar tombstones and patches of green coconut "grass" give these brownies a graveyard look.

INGREDIENTS
1 package (21.5 ounces) brownie mix, plus ingredients to prepare mix
1 cup chocolate fudge frosting (about ½ of 16-ounce container)
2 milk chocolate candy bars (1.55 ounces each)
White decorating icing
¾ cup flaked coconut, tinted green*
12 pumpkin candies

*See Tinting Coconut, page 5.

1. Preheat oven to 350°F. Line 13×9-inch baking pan with foil, extending foil beyond edges of pan; grease foil.

2. Prepare brownie mix according to package directions. Spread in prepared pan.

3. Bake 30 to 35 minutes (do not overbake). Cool in pan on wire rack.

continued

Tombstone Brownies *continued*

4. Using foil as handles, remove brownies from pan; peel off foil. Frost with chocolate frosting. Cut brownies into twelve 4×2-inch bars. Break chocolate bars into pieces along scored lines. Using white decorating icing, write R.I.P. on chocolate pieces. Let stand until set. Press 1 chocolate piece into end of each brownie as shown in photo.

5. Sprinkle tinted coconut in upper corner of each brownie for grass. Place 1 pumpkin candy on coconut.

Makes 12 servings

Black Cat Fudge

You'll welcome these rich black cats crossing your path!

**8 ounces semisweet
    chocolate, coarsely
    chopped**
¼ cup butter or margarine
⅓ cup light corn syrup
¼ cup whipping cream
1 teaspoon vanilla
¼ teaspoon salt
**16 ounces (1 pound)
    confectioners' sugar
    (about 4½ cups), sifted**
**Vanilla milk chips
    (about 30)**

1. Line 11×7-inch pan with foil, extending foil beyond edges of pan; grease foil.

2. Melt chocolate and butter in medium saucepan over low heat; stir in corn syrup, cream, vanilla and salt. Remove from heat and gradually stir in confectioners' sugar until smooth.

3. Spread evenly in prepared pan. Refrigerate until firm, 1 to 2 hours.

4. Using foil as handles, remove fudge from pan; peel off foil. Using diagram as guide, cut out cats (see Making Patterns, page 3).* Frequently clean knife with warm water and dry thoroughly to prevent sticking. Place 2 vanilla milk chips on each cat for eyes. Using knife, score feet to make claws. Cover; refrigerate until ready to serve.

*Makes about 1½ pounds
    (12 to 15 cats)*

*Fudge may also be cut with cookie cutters or into squares.

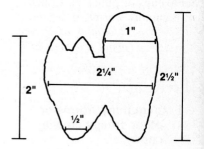

From top to bottom: *Tombstone Brownies (page 22); Black Cat Fudge*

Full-Moon Pumpkin Cheesecake

The moon is really made of cream cheese—with a touch of pumpkin and chocolate!

Gingersnap Cookie Crust (recipe follows)
4 packages (8 ounces *each*) cream cheese, softened
½ cup sugar
6 eggs
1 cup sour cream
1 cup solid pack pumpkin
2 tablespoons all-purpose flour
2 teaspoons ground cinnamon
½ teaspoon ground ginger
½ teaspoon ground allspice
3 ounces semisweet chocolate, melted
1 recipe Black Cat Fudge (page 24)

1. Prepare Gingersnap Cookie Crust; set aside.

2. *Increase oven temperature to 425°F.* Beat cream cheese in large bowl until fluffy; beat in sugar and eggs, one at a time. Add sour cream, pumpkin, flour and spices; beat well. Pour 2 cups batter into small bowl; stir in chocolate.

3. Pour remaining batter into prepared crust. Spoon chocolate batter in large swirls over batter in pan; draw knife through mixture to marbleize.

4. Bake 15 minutes. *Reduce oven temperature to 300°F.* Bake 45 minutes (center of cheesecake will not be set). Turn oven off; let cheesecake stand in oven with door slightly ajar 1 hour. Cool to room temperature in pan on wire rack. Cover; refrigerate in pan overnight.

5. Prepare Black Cat Fudge; do not cut. Using diagram as guide, cut out witch shape (see Making Patterns, page 3). Using knife, score as shown in photo. Cut small star shapes from scraps with cutter or sharp knife.

6. Remove side of pan; place cheesecake on serving plate. With wide metal spatula, carefully position witch on cheesecake as shown in photo. Position stars as shown.
   Makes 1 (9-inch) cheesecake (about 15 servings)

Gingersnap Cookie Crust

1 cup gingersnap cookie crumbs
½ cup chopped pecans
¼ cup butter or margarine, melted

1. Preheat oven to 350°F. Combine cookie crumbs and nuts in small bowl. Mix in butter.

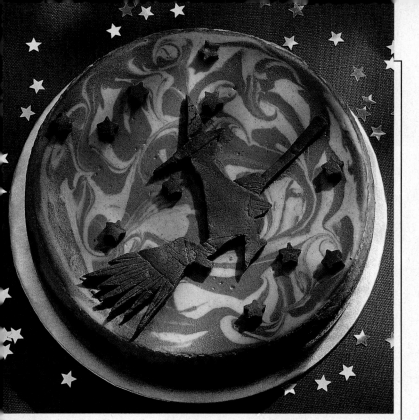

Full-Moon Pumpkin Cheesecake

2. Press mixture evenly on
bottom and 1 inch up side of
9-inch springform pan.

3. Bake 8 minutes; cool on wire
rack.   *Makes 1 crust*

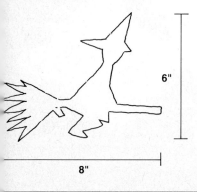

6"

8"

Spooky Ghost Cookies

*These haunting ghost cookies are
not only scrumptious, they're
"boo"-tiful!*

**1 recipe Butter Cookie
    dough (page 93)**
**1 recipe Fluffy White
    Frosting (page 93)**
**½ cup semisweet chocolate
    chips (about 60 chips)**

1. Preheat oven to 350°F. Roll
dough on floured surface to
¼-inch thickness. Using diagram
on page 29 as guide, cut out
ghost shapes (see Making
Patterns, page 3).   *continued*

Spooky Ghost Cookies *continued*

2. Bake on ungreased cookie sheets 10 to 12 minutes until edges begin to brown. Remove to wire racks; cool completely.

3. Prepare Fluffy White Frosting. Spread frosting over cookies, swirling to give ghostly appearance. Position 2 chocolate chips on each cookie for eyes.

Makes about 2 1/2 dozen cookies

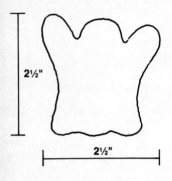

2½"

2½"

Things That Go Bump in the Night...

Each recipe makes just one scary creation so mix and match to make as many as needed.

BLOODSHOT EYEBALLS

**2 fudge-covered chocolate
    sandwich cookies
1 tablespoon Fluffy White
    Frosting (page 93)
2 green jelly beans
    Red decorating gel**

Top to bottom: *Things That Go Bump in the Night . . .; Spooky Ghost Cookies (page 27)*

Frost cookies with Fluffy White Frosting leaving edge of cookie showing as shown in photo. Press jelly beans into frosting to make pupils of eyes. Decorate with red gel to make eyes look bloodshot as shown.

SPIDERS

**1 (3-inch) oatmeal cookie
1 tablespoon Fluffy White
    Frosting (page 93)
1 small black jelly bean
1 large black jelly bean
1 black licorice whip
2 red candy-coated licorice
    pieces**

Frost oatmeal cookie with Fluffy White Frosting. Arrange jelly beans on cookies to make spider head and body as shown in photo. Cut 6 to 8 licorice whip pieces (about 1½ inches long); curve and position for legs. Add red candy antennae to head as shown.

FUNNY BUG

**1 (3-inch) oatmeal cookie
1 tablespoon Fluffy White
    Frosting (page 93)
2 miniature chocolate
    sandwich cookies
1 red gumdrop
2 cheese corn curls**

Frost oatmeal cookie with Fluffy White Frosting. Arrange sandwich cookies to make eyes as shown in photo. Attach gumdrop mouth and corn curl antennae.

THANKSGIVING

Tuxedo Turkey

Dressing for dinner takes on a whole new meaning when the Tuxedo Turkey arrives at the table!

1 turkey (14 to 16 pounds)
1 refrigerated pie crust
   (½ of 15-ounce package)
1 egg yolk
1 teaspoon water
   Red food color
   Black paste food color*

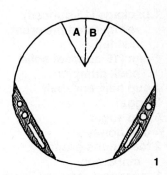

1. Roast turkey as desired. Remove from oven.

2. Preheat oven to 425°F.

3. Roll pie crust on floured surface into 12-inch circle. Cut as shown in diagram 1.

4. Carefully place large piece of crust on turkey as shown in photo. Trim to fit, if necessary. Moisten and place bow tie, buttons and trim on crust as shown in diagram 2.

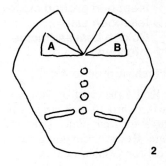

5. Combine egg yolk and water; divide into 2 small bowls. Color one red and the other black. Using small pastry brush, paint bow tie red and buttons, trim and edge of crust black. Bake 15 to 17 minutes until pastry is golden brown.

   Makes 12 to 14 servings

*Black paste food color is available at stores carrying cake decorating supplies.

Tuxedo Turkey

Golden Leaf Pumpkin Pie

Sinfully rich and perfectly spiced, this pumpkin pie is topped with a pile of golden-glazed leaves.

- **1 package (15 ounces) refrigerated pie crust, divided**
- **1 can (16 ounces) solid pack pumpkin**
- **1 cup half-and-half**
- **3 eggs**
- **⅔ cup sugar**
- **¼ cup honey**
- **2 teaspoons ground cinnamon**
- **1 teaspoon ground allspice**
- **1 teaspoon ground nutmeg**
- **½ teaspoon ground ginger**
- **½ teaspoon ground cloves**
- **½ teaspoon salt**
- **Golden Leaves (recipe follows)**

1. Preheat oven to 425°F.

2. Roll 1 pie crust on floured surface into 10-inch circle; ease into 9-inch pie plate. Trim and flute. Reserve remaining pie crust for Golden Leaves.

3. Combine remaining ingredients except Golden Leaves. Pour into crust.

4. Bake 10 minutes. *Reduce oven temperature to 350°F.* Bake 40 to 45 minutes until pastry is brown and knife inserted in center comes out clean. Cool. Garnish with Golden Leaves. Refrigerate leftovers.

Makes 8 to 10 servings

Golden Leaves

- **1 refrigerated pie crust, reserved from pie**
- **½ cup half-and-half**
- **3 tablespoons sugar**

1. Roll pastry on floured surface to ⅛-inch thickness. Using diagram as a guide, cut out leaf shapes (see Making Patterns, page 3). Mark veins in leaves with tip of knife. Roll pastry scraps into rope ¼-inch thick. Cut into 2- to 3-inch pieces and twist to make tendrils.

2. Preheat oven to 400°F. Lay pastry leaves on bottom of inverted flat-bottomed ovenproof bowl so that leaves will have a curved shape.* Lay tendrils on ungreased baking sheet. Brush leaves and tendrils with half-and-half; sprinkle with sugar. Bake 10 to 15 minutes or until golden brown. Remove to wire rack; cool completely.

Makes about 12 leaves

*Leaves may also be baked flat on ungreased baking sheet.

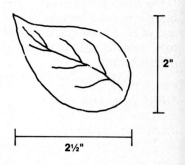

2"

2½"

Golden Leaf Pumpkin Pie

Wassail Bowl

Sugared apple shapes float atop this classic spiced punch to give it a pretty look.

INGREDIENTS

Dried apple slices
Colored sugar
¾ cup water
¾ cup granulated sugar
½ teaspoon ground ginger
¼ teaspoon ground nutmeg
1 small cinnamon stick
3 whole cloves
3 whole allspice
3 coriander seeds
3 cardamom seeds (optional)
3 cups ale or wine
2¼ cups dry sherry
⅓ cup cognac

SUPPLIES

Tiny cookie cutters

1. Using tiny cookie cutters or sharp knife, cut dried apple slices into festive shapes; moisten with water and coat with colored sugar. Set aside.

2. Combine ¾ cup water, granulated sugar and spices in large saucepan. Bring to a boil. Cover; reduce heat and simmer 5 minutes.

3. Stir in ale, sherry and cognac; heat just to simmering. *Do not boil.* Strain into heatproof punch bowl. Float apple slices in punch.   *Makes 12 servings (about 4 ounces each)*

Give Thanks Cornucopias

Great favors for kids that can be filled with all sorts of goodies.

INGREDIENTS

8 ice cream sugar cones
3 ounces semisweet chocolate, melted
Assorted fall candies

SUPPLIES (optional)

8 (2 × ¾-inch) pieces lightweight cardboard

1. Dip edges of cones into melted chocolate; let stand on wire racks or waxed paper until chocolate is firm. Place each cone on its side as shown in photo; fill with candy.

2. To make place cards, write names on pieces of cardboard. Attach to top of cones with melted chocolate as shown.
    Makes 8 favors or place cards

Cookie Gobblers

These gobblers make charming place card holders or a simple kids' dessert.

INGREDIENTS

8 marshmallow puff cookies
4 striped shortbread ring cookies
¼ cup semisweet chocolate chips, melted
8 candy corn

From left to right: *Give Thanks Cornucopias; Cookie Gobblers*

SUPPLIES (optional)
8 (2½×1½-inch) pieces lightweight cardboard

1. Cut down into marshmallow cookie halfway between center and edge as shown in diagram. Starting in back, cut horizontally toward first cut. Dip knife in hot water and dry it before each cut. Discard piece.

2. Cut striped cookies in half. Attach 1 striped cookie half with melted chocolate to cut edge of marshmallow cookie to form tail as shown in photo. Attach candy corn to front of turkey with melted chocolate as shown. Repeat with remaining cookies.

3. To make place cards, write names near top edges of cardboard. Place behind striped cookie half; attach with melted chocolate, if desired.

Makes 8 turkeys

side view

35

From top to bottom: *Centerpiece Cornucopia; Braided Bread Napkin Rings*

Centerpiece Cornucopia

A beautiful centerpiece for your Thanksgiving table, this cornucopia can be filled with fresh fruit or an assortment of fresh-baked breads or rolls.

INGREDIENTS

  1 package (16 ounces)
    hot roll mix, plus
      ingredients to prepare
      mix
  2 egg yolks
  1 tablespoon cold water
    Assorted fresh fruit

SUPPLIES

  1 (16 × 14-inch) piece
    lightweight cardboard

1. To make cornucopia mold, shape cardboard into cone shape. The large open end of cone should measure about 6 inches in diameter. Tape securely. Trim if necessary. Cover outside of cone with foil; grease.

2. Prepare hot roll mix according to package directions. Knead dough on lightly floured surface until smooth, about 5 minutes. Cover loosely; let stand in bowl about 15 minutes.

3. Grease cookie sheet. Set aside $1/8$ of dough. Roll and stretch remaining dough on lightly floured surface into triangle as shown in diagram. Shape reserved dough into 28- to 30-inch rope (about $1/2$ inch thick).

4. Shape dough triangle around cone, pinching seam on bottom to seal. At point of cornucopia, stretch dough 3 to 4 inches and form a loop, pinching to top of cornucopia to seal.

5. Press dough rope around opening of cornucopia in decorative pattern. Insert wooden toothpicks at 2 inch intervals to hold rope in place during baking. Cover loosely; let rise in warm place until doubled in size, about 30 minutes.

6. Preheat oven to 350°F. Combine egg yolks and water; brush over cornucopia. Bake 20 to 25 minutes or until golden. Remove to wire rack; cool completely. Remove wooden toothpicks. Carefully remove cardboard mold, if desired. Fill with assorted fresh fruit.

Makes 1 cornucopia

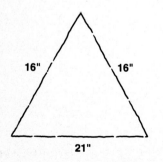

16" / \ 16"

21"

Braided Bread Napkin Rings

Homemade napkin rings will bring country charm to your holiday table.

INGREDIENTS

1 package (16 ounces) hot roll mix, plus ingredients to prepare mix
1 egg yolk
1 tablespoon cold water

SUPPLIES

4 paper tubes from paper towels, foil or other wrap

1. Wrap tubes in foil; grease lightly. Grease baking sheets.

2. Prepare hot roll mix according to package directions. Knead dough on floured surface until smooth. Cover loosely; let stand in bowl about 15 minutes.

3. Roll dough on lightly floured surface into two 12×6-inch rectangles. Cut dough into strips (6×$1/2$ inch) to make 48 strips.

4. Braid 3 strips of dough. Wrap around prepared tubes, pinching ends of dough to seal. Repeat with remaining dough. Place on prepared baking sheets. Cover loosely; let rise until double in size, about 30 minutes.

5. Preheat oven to 375°F. Combine egg yolk and water; carefully brush on dough.

continued

Braided Bread Napkin Rings
continued
6. Bake 10 to 12 minutes or until golden. Remove tubes to wire racks; cool completely on tubes. Carefully remove rings.

Makes 16 napkin rings

Note: If making less than 16 napkin rings, remaining dough can be shaped into rolls and baked according to package directions.

Pretzel Log Cabin

Pretzels and other store-bought snacks transform an ordinary box into a memorable centerpiece.

INGREDIENTS
- **3 egg whites**
- **3 cups confectioners' sugar**
  Decorations: Pretzel rods, pretzel sticks, pretzel twists, corn nuts, shredded wheat biscuit cereal, nuts, crackers banana chips and assorted dried fruits
- **1 Cookie Gobbler, optional (page 34)**
- **2 cups shredded coconut, tinted green***

SUPPLIES
- **1 (6×6×8-inch) cardboard box**
- **1 (13×11-inch) cake board, covered, or large tray**

1. To make house, cut flaps off bottom of box. Stand box on cake board; tape in place. Fold 2 top flaps of box up to form roof; tape together. Cut triangular gables from bottom flaps; tape into place. Cover box with foil.

2. Beat egg whites in medium bowl until fluffy; gradually beat in sugar. Keep frosting in bowl covered with a damp towel while working. Frost 1 side of house with frosting; decorate as shown in photo. Repeat with remaining sides and roof.   *Makes 1 cabin*

*See Tinting Coconut, page 5.

Note: Pretzel logs and sticks may need to be trimmed to fit. Cut carefully with sharp knife.

Pretzel Log Cabin

Autumn Mobile

This colorful mobile can hang over the dinner table or in a doorway. For a fun party favor, personalize each cookie with piping gel and let the guests snip their cookie off the mobile as they leave.

INGREDIENTS

1 recipe Butter Cookie dough (page 93)
3 egg yolks
3 teaspoons water
Yellow, red and green food color

SUPPLIES

Plastic drinking straw
Small brush
Ribbon or yarn

1. Preheat oven to 350°F.

2. Roll dough on floured surface to ¼-inch thickness. Using diagrams as guides, cut out 1 large pumpkin cookie, 2 leaf cookies and 3 small pumpkin cookies (see Making Patterns, page 3). Cut out remaining dough as desired.

3. Place large pumpkin cookie on ungreased cookie sheet. Place remaining cookies on another ungreased cookie sheet. Using plastic straw, make hole in top of each pumpkin cookie, about ½ inch from top. Make holes in sides of leaf cookies. Make 3 evenly spaced holes along bottom edge of large cookie, about ½ inch from edge.

Autumn Mobile

4. Place 1 egg yolk in each of 3 separate bowls. Add 1 teaspoon water to each; beat lightly. Color egg wash in 1 bowl orange,* another yellow and the last green. Using a small brush, decorate cookies as shown in photo.

5. Bake smaller cookies 10 to 12 minutes until lightly brown around edges. Bake large cookie about 14 minutes. Remove to wire racks; cool completely.

6. Using ribbon, tie cookies together as shown. For ease in balancing mobile, tie large pumpkin cookie to cabinet handle while tying on other cookies. *Makes 1 mobile and 1 dozen cookies*

*Use about 1 drop red food color to every 3 drops yellow to make orange color.

Note: *Extra cookie dough may be used to make additional mobiles.*

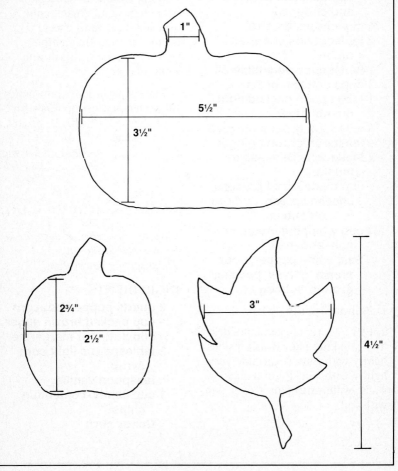

Cheesy Squash Soup

Eat the bowl as part of the meal! With each spoonful, be sure to include some of the cooked squash with the soup.

4 small acorn squash, cut into halves, seeded
Butter or margarine, softened
Salt
2 medium Granny Smith apples, peeled, cored and chopped
⅔ cup chopped carrot
2 tablespoons chopped onion
1 tablespoon vegetable oil
3 cups chicken broth
1 tablespoon packed light brown sugar
¼ teaspoon ground allspice
⅛ teaspoon ground ginger
2 teaspoons Dijon-style mustard
1 cup pasteurized process cheese spread, cut into ½-inch cubes
¼ cup whipping cream or half-and-half
Salt, white pepper, sour cream, chives, pecans, ground nutmeg

1. Preheat oven to 400°F.

2. Place acorn squash, cut sides up, in baking pan. Brush insides lightly with butter; sprinkle very lightly with salt. Pour ¼ inch warm water into pan. Cover pan with foil.

3. Bake, covered, 35 to 40 minutes until squash is tender.

4. Cook apples, carrot and onion in hot oil in large saucepan over medium-high heat 5 to 7 minutes until onion is tender. Add chicken broth; bring to a boil. Reduce heat; cover and simmer 20 minutes. Stir in sugar, spices and mustard.

5. Process apple mixture in blender or food processor until smooth. Return to saucepan. Add cheese and cream; cook over low heat until cheese is melted, stirring frequently. Season to taste with salt and white pepper.

6. Place squash halves on plates; fill centers with soup. Garnish with sour cream, chives, pecans and nutmeg.

*Makes 8 servings
(about ½ cup each)*

Indian Caramel Corn

Easy-to-make ears of corn are a festive addition to any Thanksgiving celebration.

INGREDIENTS
2 quarts popped popcorn
½ cup packed brown sugar
¼ cup butter or margarine
2 tablespoons light corn syrup
¼ teaspoon vanilla
1 cup candy-coated fun chips
Candy corn

Indian Caramel Corn

SUPPLIES

Parchment paper, tan raffia or waxed paper

1. Place popped popcorn in large buttered bowl.

2. Combine brown sugar, butter, corn syrup and vanilla in small saucepan. Bring to a boil. Boil 1 minute.

3. Pour sugar mixture over popcorn; stir to coat evenly. Sprinkle with fun chips; stir well.

4. Lightly butter hands. Shape about $1/2$ cup mixture into tapered oval about 4 inches long to resemble ear of corn. Press candy corn into ear of corn as shown in photo. Place on waxed paper to cool. Repeat with remaining mixture.

5. Cut parchment paper into twelve 6-inch squares. Roll into cone shape and fringe ends by cutting into strips. Insert into ends of corn with tip of sharp knife.

Makes about 12 ears of corn

Fall Harvest Spice Cake

Celebrate harvest time with this tempting spice cake topped with sweet, creamy maple frosting and lots of nuts and fruits.

- **1 package (18.25 ounces) spice or carrot cake mix**
- **1 cup water**
- **3 eggs**
- **⅓ cup vegetable oil**
- **⅓ cup apple butter**
- **Maple Buttercream Frosting (recipe follows)**
- **2 cups coarsely chopped walnuts**
- **¼ cup semisweet chocolate chips, melted**
- **¼ cup chopped almonds**
- **2 tablespoons chopped dried apricots**
- **2 tablespoons chopped dried cranberries***
- **2 tablespoons raisins**

1. Preheat oven to 375°F. Grease and flour two 9-inch round baking pans.

2. Combine cake mix, water, eggs, oil and apple butter in medium bowl. Beat at low speed of electric mixer until blended; beat at medium speed 2 minutes. Pour batter into prepared pans.

3. Bake 35 to 40 minutes until wooden toothpick inserted into center comes out clean. Let cool in pans on wire rack 10 minutes. Remove to racks; cool completely.

4. Prepare Maple Buttercream Frosting.

5. Place 1 cake layer on serving plate; frost top with Maple Buttercream. Top with second layer; frost top and side of cake with frosting. Press walnuts into side of cake.

6. Pipe chocolate onto cake for tree trunk as shown in photo (see Piping Chocolate, page 5). Combine almonds, apricots, cranberries and raisins. Sprinkle on top of cake as shown.

Makes 12 servings

*If dried cranberries are unavailable use additional chopped dried apricots and raisins.

Maple Buttercream Frosting

- **4 tablespoons butter or margarine, softened**
- **¼ cup maple or pancake syrup**
- **3 cups confectioners' sugar**

In small bowl, beat butter and syrup until blended. Gradually beat in confectioners' sugar until smooth.   *Makes about 3 cups*

Fall Harvest Spice Cake

Spiced Red Wine with Grape Ice Ring

Spiced Red Wine

The Grape Ice Ring adds a special touch to this traditional fall beverage.

Grape Ice Ring (recipe follows)
½ **cup sugar**
½ **cup water**
1 **bottle Burgundy wine, chilled**
2 **cups white grape juice, chilled**
1 **cup peach schnapps, chilled**

1. Prepare Grape Ice Ring.

2. Combine sugar and water in a small saucepan. Bring to a boil. Boil, stirring constantly, until sugar is dissolved. Cool to room temperature. Cover; refrigerate until chilled, about 2 hours.

3. Combine wine, grape juice, schnapps and sugar syrup in punch bowl. Float Grape Ice Ring in punch.

Makes 14 servings
(about 4 ounces each)

46

Grape Ice Ring

INGREDIENTS

**2 pounds assorted
 seedless grapes
 (Thompson, Red
 Empress, etc.)**

SUPPLIES
 Lemon leaves,* optional

Fill 4-cup ring mold with water to within ¾ inch of top. Freeze until firm, about 8 hours or overnight. Arrange clusters of grapes and leaves on ice as shown in photo; fill with water to top of mold. Freeze until solid, about 6 hours. To unmold, dip bottom of mold briefly in hot water.

*These nontoxic leaves are available in florist shops.

***Note:** Spiced Red Wine is also delicious served hot. Omit ice ring. Heat all ingredients in medium saucepan.* Do not boil. *Serve immediately.*

Family Friendship Praline

An oversized praline makes a fabulous gift and is designed to be broken into pieces and shared with family and friends.

1 cup pecan halves
**½ cup butter (*do not use
 margarine*)**
⅓ cup granulated sugar
**⅓ cup packed light brown
 sugar**
**1 tablespoon light corn
 syrup**
1 teaspoon vanilla

1. Line 8-inch round pan with foil, extending foil beyond edges of pan; butter foil lightly.

2. Combine pecans, butter, sugars and corn syrup in medium saucepan. Bring to a boil over medium heat. Boil, stirring constantly, about 5 minutes or until mixture turns golden brown. Remove from heat; stir in vanilla.

3. Pour mixture into prepared pan and spread evenly. Cool completely on wire rack.

4. Remove praline from pan using foil as handles; peel off foil.   *Makes 6 to 8 servings*

CHRISTMAS

Merry Christmas Present Cake

An eye catching marzipan bow transforms an everyday looking cake into a dazzling gift box.

1 recipe Marzipan (page 93)
Red food color
1 package (18.25 ounces) devil's food cake mix
1 cup water
½ cup vegetable oil
3 eggs
1 teaspoon vanilla
3 tablespoons unsweetened cocoa
1 cup mini chocolate chips
⅔ cup finely ground hazelnuts or almonds
1 cup whipping cream
2 tablespoons butter or margarine
6 ounces semisweet chocolate, coarsely chopped

1. Prepare Marzipan, coloring it red as shown in photo, set aside.

2. Preheat oven to 350°F. Grease and flour 13×9-inch pan.

3. Combine cake mix, water, oil, eggs, vanilla and cocoa in large bowl. Beat on low speed of electric mixer until blended; beat at medium speed 2 minutes. Mix in chocolate chips and nuts. Pour batter into prepared pan.

4. Bake 50 to 60 minutes or until wooden toothpick inserted into center of cake comes out clean. Cool in pan on wire rack 15 minutes. Remove from pan and cool completely on rack.

5. Bring cream and butter to a simmer in small saucepan; remove from heat. Add chopped chocolate, stirring until melted. Cool to room temperature. Cover; refrigerate until mixture is thick enough to spread, about 1½ hours.

6. Place cake on serving tray. Frost with thickened chocolate mixture. Refrigerate until cake is well chilled, about 2 hours.

7. Divide marzipan into 4 equal parts. Roll 1 part into ½-inch-thick rope. Place rope between sheets of waxed paper and roll into strip 1-inch wide and 16 to 18 inches long (use sharp knife to make edges straight).

8. Lay strip lengthwise down center of cake continuing down over sides; trim ends to fit. Repeat rolling procedure with second piece of marzipan; cut crosswise in half. Place strips on cake as shown in diagram on page 50; trim ends.

continued

Merry Christmas Present Cake

49

Merry Christmas Present Cake
continued

9. Repeat rolling procedure with third piece of marzipan, making strip 15 inches long. Fold ends in toward center to make bottom loops of bow as shown in diagram 2; place on cake as shown. Repeat rolling procedure with fourth piece of marzipan, making one 8-inch strip and one 4-inch strip. Cut 8-inch strip in half crosswise; fold into 2 loops and place on first loop as shown in diagram 2. Fold under ends of 4-inch strip to form loop; place as shown in diagram 2.

Makes 12 to 16 servings

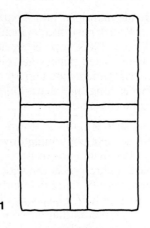

Heavenly Angels

These adorable angles can be grouped to form a heavenly choir, used to decorate a cake or given away as take-home favors.

6 tablespoons Marzipan (page 93)
3 white chocolate baking bars (2 ounces *each*) or confectionery coating, coarsely chopped
6 ice cream sugar cones Assorted colored sugars and sprinkles
6 large pretzel twists Assorted food colors
⅓ cup shredded coconut, tinted yellow*
6 small (about 1½ inches) round cookies

1. Prepare Marzipan; set aside.

2. Melt white chocolate in top of double boiler over hot, not boiling, water. Using spoon or pastry brush, coat 1 ice cream cone at a time with melted white chocolate. Dip cone in colored sugar and decorate with sprinkles as shown in photo. Place on waxed paper-lined baking sheet; refrigerate until firm.

3. Dip pretzels in white chocolate, turning with fork to coat completely. Remove to

*See Tinting Coconut, page 5.

Heavenly Angels

waxed paper-lined baking sheet. Refrigerate until firm. Reserve remaining white chocolate.

4. To form angel's head, roll about 1 tablespoon marzipan into smooth ball; repeat to make 6 heads. Paint features on heads as shown in photo with wooden toothpicks and cotton swabs dipped in food color.

5. Press marzipan heads onto pointed ends of cones. Attach pretzel wings to back of cone bodies with some of reserved melted white chocolate, remelting chocolate if necessary. For best appearance, attach smooth side of pretzels to body.

6. Attach tinted coconut hair and cookie halos to heads with melted white chocolate as shown. Refrigerate until firm.

Makes 6 angels

Festive Popcorn Treats

Kids love this Christmas version of popcorn balls. The peanut butter adds a great flavor twist.

6 cups popped popcorn
½ cup sugar
½ cup light corn syrup
¼ cup peanut butter
Green food color
¼ cup red cinnamon candies

1. Line baking sheet with waxed paper. Pour popcorn into large bowl.

2. Combine sugar and corn syrup in medium saucepan. Bring to a boil over medium heat, stirring constantly; boil 1 minute. Remove from heat.

3. Add peanut butter and green food color; stir until peanut butter is completely melted. Pour over popcorn; stir to coat well.

4. Lightly butter hands and shape popcorn mixture into trees as shown in photo. While trees are still warm, press red cinnamon candies into trees. Place on prepared baking sheet; let stand until firm, about 30 minutes.   *Makes 6 servings*

Tiger Stripes

The streaks of white and dark chocolate on top of this decadent candy resemble tiger stripes.

1 package (12 ounces) semisweet chocolate chips
3 tablespoons chunky peanut butter, divided
2 white chocolate baking bars (2 ounces *each*)

1. Line 8×8-inch square pan with foil. Grease lightly.

2. Melt semisweet chocolate with 2 tablespoons peanut butter in small saucepan over low heat; stir well.

3. Pour half of chocolate mixture into prepared pan. Let stand 10 to 15 minutes to cool slightly.

4. Melt white baking bar with remaining 1 tablespoon peanut butter in small saucepan over low heat. Spoon half of white chocolate mixture over dark chocolate mixture. Drop remaining dark and white chocolate mixtures by spoonfuls over mixture in pan.

5. Using small metal spatula or knife, pull through the chocolates to create tiger stripes.

6. Freeze about 1 hour or until firm. Remove from pan; peel off foil. Cut into 36 pieces. Refrigerate until ready to serve.
          Makes 36 pieces

Clockwise from top left: Festive Popcorn Treats; Good Luck Meringue Mushrooms in Cherished Chocolate Boxes (page 54); Tiger Stripes

Cherished Chocolate Boxes

For an extra-special gift, fill these easy-to-make chocolate boxes with all sorts of Christmas goodies. For variety, try different sizes and shapes of foil pans.

INGREDIENTS
24 ounces milk or semisweet confectionery coating, chopped

SUPPLIES
Pastry brush
4 (5¾ × 3¼-inch) mini foil loaf pans

1. Melt chocolate coating in top of double boiler over hot, not boiling, water.

2. Brush melted chocolate with pastry brush in thin layer inside each foil pan, covering bottom and sides. Refrigerate until chocolate is firm. (Keep pastry brush wrapped in plastic wrap while chocolate is chilling.)

3. Brush another layer of chocolate over first; refrigerate. Repeat layers until chocolate is about ¼-inch thick (you should use all the melted chocolate). Cover with plastic wrap; refrigerate 1 hour to ensure that chocolate is firm throughout.

4. Snip rims of foil pans at ½-inch intervals with scissors. Carefully peel off foil pans. Fill boxes with Good Luck Meringue Mushrooms or other treats. *Makes 4 boxes*

Good Luck Meringue Mushrooms

In European tradition, mushroom cookies are served from a basket and given to each guest as a good luck symbol at holiday time.

INGREDIENTS
2 egg whites
Pinch cream of tartar
½ cup sugar
½ cup semisweet chocolate chips, melted
Unsweetened cocoa

SUPPLIES
Parchment paper
Pastry bag and large writing tip

1. Preheat oven to 250°F. Beat egg whites in small bowl until foamy. Add cream of tartar and beat until soft peaks form. Add sugar, 2 tablespoons at a time, beating until stiff and glossy.

2. Line baking sheets with parchment paper. Spoon mixture into pastry bag fitted with large writing tip. Pipe 1-inch rounds to make mushroom caps. Smooth tops with wet fingertips. Pipe 1-inch-high cones to make stems. (Pipe an equal number of caps and cones.)

3. Bake about 30 minutes or until firm. Turn oven off; let stand in oven 1 hour. Remove from oven; cool completely.

4. Make small hole in center of flat side of each cap with sharp

knife. Fill hole with melted chocolate. Insert stem into hole. Set aside until chocolate sets.

5. Sift cocoa through fine sieve over mushroom caps. Serve in Cherished Chocolate Box, if desired.

Makes about 2½ dozen cookies

Note: *These can be made ahead and stored, loosely covered, at room temperature for up to a week. Avoid making these cookies on humid days as they may become moist and sticky.*

Chocolate Snowflakes

Paper snowflakes—the kind you used to make as a child—act as stencils to create snowy sugar patterns atop these good cookies.

INGREDIENTS
   1 recipe Chocolate Cookie dough (page 92)
   Confectioners' sugar

SUPPLIES
   3-inch round cookie cutter
   Parchment paper

1. Preheat oven to 325°F. Grease cookie sheets.

2. Roll dough on floured surface to ⅛-inch thickness. Using 3-inch cookie cutter, cut into circles. Place 1 inch apart on prepared cookie sheets.

3. Bake 8 to 10 minutes until edges begin to brown. Remove to wire racks; cool completely.

4. To make snowflakes, cut several pieces of parchment paper into 3-inch circles. Fold each in half, then into quarters. With scissors, cut small pieces from folded edges to create snowflake design.

5. Unfold circles and place on top of cooled cookies. Sift confectioners' sugar generously over paper patterns. Carefully remove paper. Repeat with remaining cookies.

Makes about 2 dozen

Gingerbread Folks

Give ordinary gingerbread people more personality by bending their arms and legs into dancing poses before baking.

INGREDIENTS
   1 recipe Gingerbread Cookie dough (page 92)
   Assorted food colors
   Vanilla frosting and assorted decorating gels
   Assorted candies and decorations

SUPPLIES
   6-inch gingerbread boy and girl cookie cutters

1. Preheat oven to 350°F. Grease cookie sheets.

continued

Gingerbread Folks *continued*

2. Roll dough on floured surface to ⅛-inch thickness. Cut out cookies with cookie cutters. Place on prepared cookie sheets. Bend arms and legs to make cookies look like they're dancing.

3. Bake 8 to 10 minutes or until edges begin to brown. Remove to wire racks; cool completely.

4. Color frosting as desired. Decorate as shown in photo.
    Makes about 6 large cookies

Note: Gingerbread Folks can also be made into ornaments. See Kittens and Mittens (page 76) for complete directions.

Lollipop Cookies

A whimsical treat formed by sandwiching a luscious chocolate filling between two butter cookies.

INGREDIENTS

  2 recipes Butter Cookie dough (page 93)
  1 cup semisweet chocolate chips, melted
  ½ cup finely chopped hazelnuts or almonds
  1 cup vanilla frosting (about ½ of 16 ounce container)
  Red and green decorating gel
  Colored sugars

SUPPLIES

  2-inch round cookie cutter
  24 (4-inch) lollipop sticks*

1. Preheat oven to 350°F. Grease cookie sheets.

2. Roll dough on floured surface to ¼-inch thickness. Cut out 48 circles using cookie cutter. Place 24 circles on prepared cookie sheets.

3. Combine melted chocolate and hazelnuts. Spoon rounded ½ teaspoon chocolate mixture in center of each dough circle on cookie sheet. Place lollipop sticks on circle so that tips of sticks are imbedded in filling. Top with remaining dough circles; seal edges of dough together with floured fork tines.

4. Bake 10 to 12 minutes until edges begin to brown. Remove to wire racks; cool completely.

5. Frost tops and sides of cookies with vanilla frosting. Decorate with decorating gel and colored sugars as shown in photo.
    Makes 2 dozen sandwich cookies

*Lollipop sticks are available at stores carrying cake decorating supplies.

Clockwise from left: *Lollipop Cookies; Gingerbread Folks (page 55); Chocolate Snowflakes (page 55)*

Sweet Potato Wreaths

Traditional sweet potatoes add extra charm to your holiday dinner when you pipe them into decorative wreath shapes.

INGREDIENTS

1 can (40 ounces) sweet potatoes or yams, drained
⅓ cup apricot jam
2 eggs
1 teaspoon Dijon mustard
1 teaspoon cider vinegar
¼ cup packed light brown sugar
¼ cup all-purpose flour
½ teaspoon ground ginger
½ teaspoon salt
¼ teaspoon ground white pepper
12 dried apricot halves, cut into fourths
12 candied green cherries, cut into halves

SUPPLIES

Pastry bag and large star tip

1. Preheat oven to 400°F. Grease baking sheets.

2. Beat sweet potatoes in medium bowl until smooth; beat in jam, eggs, mustard and vinegar. Combine brown sugar, flour, ginger, salt and pepper; stir into potatoes.

3. Spoon sweet potato mixture into pastry bag fitted with large star tip. Pipe into 2½-inch rings on prepared baking sheets. Place chopped apricots and cherries on wreaths for garnish.

4. Bake 8 to 10 minutes or until set and lightly brown. Remove from baking sheet carefully. Serve immediately.

Makes about 2 dozen wreaths

Yule Tree Namesakes

Make as many of these adorable place cards as needed for your holiday dinner table, then serve the remaining decorated cookies for dessert.

INGREDIENTS

1 recipe Gingerbread Cookie dough (page 92)
1 recipe Cookie Glaze (page 93)
Green food color
Confectioners' sugar
Assorted candies
3 packages (12 ounces *each*) semisweet chocolate chips, melted
1 cup flaked coconut, tinted green*

SUPPLIES

Pastry bag and small writing tip
24 foil baking cups (1¾ inches) or small foil tartlet pans (3 inches)
3½- to 4-inch tree-shaped cookie cutter

*See Tinting Coconut, page 5.

Yule Tree Namesakes

1. Preheat oven to 350°F. Roll dough on floured surface to ⅛-inch thickness. Cut out cookies using cookie cutter. Place 2 inches apart on ungreased cookie sheets.

2. Bake 12 to 14 minutes until edges begin to brown. Remove to wire racks; cool completely.

3. Reserve ⅓ cup Cookie Glaze; color remaining glaze green with food color. Place cookies on wire rack over waxed paper-lined baking sheet. Spoon green glaze over cookies.

4. Add 1 to 2 tablespoons confectioners' sugar to reserved Cookie Glaze. Spoon into pastry bag fitted with small writing tip. Pipe names onto trees as shown in photo. Decorate with assorted candies as shown. Let stand until glaze is set.

5. Spoon melted chocolate into baking cups or tartlet pans, filling evenly. Let stand until chocolate is very thick and partially set. Place trees, standing upright, in chocolate.

6. Sprinkle tinted coconut over chocolate.

Makes 24 place cards

White Chocolate Bavarian Christmas Tree

An elegant dessert, creamy and rich to delight holiday guests. If dark chocolate is more to your liking, substitute semisweet chocolate for the white.

INGREDIENTS

    1 cup half-and-half
    2 teaspoons vanilla
    2 envelopes unflavored
       gelatin
    6 eggs, separated*
   12 ounces high-quality white
       or semisweet chocolate
    1 teaspoon cream of tartar
  1½ cups whipping cream,
       whipped
       Decorations: Spearmint
       candy leaves, red
       cinnamon candies, red
       candy-coated licorice
       pieces, green miniature
       jaw breakers

SUPPLIES

       8-cup tree mold or other
       decorative mold

1. Combine half-and-half and vanilla in medium saucepan. Sprinkle gelatin over mixture; let stand 1 minute. Stir over low heat until gelatin is completely dissolved.

2. Beat egg yolks in small bowl. Stir about ½ cup gelatin mixture into egg yolks; return egg yolk mixture to saucepan. Cook over low heat, stirring constantly, until thick enough to coat the back of a spoon.

3. Melt chocolate in top of double boiler over hot, not boiling, water, stirring constantly. Stir gelatin mixture into chocolate. Remove from heat; cool to room temperature.

4. Beat egg whites and cream of tartar until stiff peaks form. Gently fold cooled chocolate mixture into beaten egg whites. Fold in whipped cream.

5. Spoon mixture into 8-cup tree or other decorative mold. Refrigerate until set, 8 hours or overnight.

6. To unmold, pull chocolate mixture from edge of mold with moistened fingers. Or, run small metal spatula or pointed knife dipped in warm water around edge of mold. Dip bottom of mold briefly in warm water. Place serving plate on top of mold. Invert mold and plate and shake to loosen chocolate mixture. Gently remove mold. Decorate with candies as shown in photo.
Makes 12 to 14 servings

*Use only grade A clean, uncracked eggs.

White Chocolate Bavarian Christmas Tree

Pesto Cheese Wreath

Smooth cream cheese, garlicky pesto and colorful roasted red peppers are layered in a ring mold to create a beautiful and delicious wreath-shaped spread.

Parsley-Basil Pesto* (recipe follows)
3 packages (8 ounces *each*) cream cheese, softened
½ cup mayonnaise
¼ cup whipping cream or half-and-half
1 teaspoon sugar
1 teaspoon onion salt
⅓ cup chopped roasted red peppers** or pimiento, drained
Pimiento strips and Italian flat leaf parsley leaves (optional)
Assorted crackers and vegetables

1. Prepare Parsley-Basil Pesto; set aside.

2. Beat cream cheese and mayonnaise in small bowl until smooth; beat in whipping cream, sugar and onion salt.

3. Line 5-cup ring mold with plastic wrap. Spoon half the cheese mixture into prepared mold; spread evenly. Spread Parsley-Basil Pesto evenly over cheese; top with chopped red peppers. Spoon remaining cheese mixture over peppers; spread evenly. Cover; refrigerate until cheese is firm, 8 hours or overnight.

4. Uncover mold; invert onto serving plate. Carefully remove plastic wrap. Smooth top and sides of wreath with spatula. Garnish with pimiento strips and parsley leaves as shown in photo, if desired. Serve with assorted crackers and vegetables.
Makes 16 to 24 servings

*One-half cup purchased pesto may be substituted for Parsley-Basil Pesto.

**Look for roasted red peppers packed in cans or jars in the Italian food section of the supermarket.

Parsley-Basil Pesto

2 cups parsley leaves
¼ cup pine nuts or slivered almonds
2 tablespoons grated Parmesan cheese
2 cloves garlic
1 tablespoon dried basil leaves
¼ teaspoon salt
2 tablespoons olive or vegetable oil

Process all ingredients except oil in food processor or blender until finely chopped. With machine running, add oil gradually, processing until mixture is smooth.
Makes about ½ cup

Clockwise from left: *Cheese Pine Cones (page 64); Holiday Appetizer Puffs (page 64); Pesto Cheese Wreath*

Cheese Pine Cones

A savory cheese spread shaped to resemble pine cones.

- **2 cups (8 ounces) shredded Swiss cheese**
- **½ cup butter or margarine, softened**
- **3 tablespoons milk**
- **2 tablespoons dry sherry or milk**
- **⅛ teaspoon ground red pepper**
- **1 cup finely chopped blanched almonds**
- **¾ cup slivered blanched almonds**
- **¾ cup sliced unblanched almonds**
- **½ cup whole unblanched almonds**
- **Fresh rosemary sprigs**

1. Beat cheese, butter, milk, sherry and red pepper in medium bowl until mixture is smooth; stir in chopped almonds.

2. Divide mixture into 3 equal portions; shape each into tapered ovals to resemble pine cones. Insert slivered, sliced and whole almonds into cones as shown in photo on page 63. Cover; refrigerate 2 to 3 hours or until firm.

3. Arrange cheese pine cones on wooden board or serving plate. Garnish tops with rosemary as shown. Serve with assorted crackers. *Makes 3 pine cones (12 to 16 servings)*

Holiday Appetizer Puffs

Ready-made puff pastry is the secret to preparing these appetizers fast. They look fussy, but actually take only minutes to prepare.

INGREDIENTS

- **1 sheet frozen puff pastry, thawed (½ of 17¼-ounce package)**
- **2 tablespoons olive or vegetable oil**
- **Toppings: grated Parmesan cheese, sesame seeds, poppy seeds, dried dill weed, dried basil, paprika, drained capers, green olive slices**

SUPPLIES

    2½- to 3-inch cookie cutters

1. Preheat oven to 425°F. Roll pastry on lightly floured surface to 13 × 13-inch square. Cut into shapes with cookie cutters (simple shaped cutters work best). Place on ungreased baking sheets.

2. Brush cut-outs lightly with oil. Decorate with desired toppings.

3. Bake 6 to 8 minutes or until golden. Serve warm or at room temperature.
Makes about 1½ dozen

From top to bottom: *Cherry Merry Christmas Crunch;*
Eggnog Gift Fudge (page 66)

Cherry Merry Christmas Crunch

The wonderful flavors of maple
and cherry meld together in this
colorful candy.

INGREDIENTS

2 cups walnut halves
1 cup candied red and
    green cherries, cut in
    half
2 tablespoons butter or
    margarine
1 teaspoon maple extract
¼ teaspoon cherry extract
1 teaspoon salt
2 cups sugar
¾ cup light corn syrup
¼ cup maple syrup

SUPPLIES

Candy thermometer

1. Generously grease baking
sheet.

2. Combine walnuts, cherries,
butter, extracts and salt in
medium bowl; set aside.

3. Combine sugar, corn syrup
and maple syrup in heavy, large
saucepan. Bring to a boil. Cook
over medium heat until mixture
reaches 300°F on candy
thermometer (hard-crack stage).

4. Remove from heat; stir in
walnut mixture. Quickly pour
onto prepared pan. Cool
completely. Break into pieces.
    Makes about 2 pounds candy

Note: *Cherry Merry Christmas*
Crunch can be made up to 1 week
ahead and stored in an airtight
container.

Eggnog Gift Fudge

A unique way to give this delightful fudge as a gift is to wrap individual squares like miniature presents.

INGREDIENTS
- ¾ **cup prepared eggnog**
- 2 **tablespoons light corn syrup**
- 2 **tablespoons butter or margarine**
- 2 **cups sugar**
- 1 **teaspoon vanilla**

SUPPLIES
- **Pastry brush**
- **Candy thermometer**
- **Ribbon bows**

1. Butter 8×8-inch pan. Lightly butter inside of heavy, medium saucepan.

2. Combine eggnog, corn syrup, butter and sugar in prepared saucepan. Cook over medium heat, stirring constantly, until sugar dissolves and mixture comes to a boil. Wash down sides of pan with pastry brush dipped frequently in hot water to remove sugar crystals.

3. Add candy thermometer. Continue to cook until mixture reaches 238°F (soft-ball stage).

4. Pour into large heatproof bowl. Cool to lukewarm (about 110°F).

5. Add vanilla; beat with heavy-duty electric mixer until thick. Spread in prepared pan. Score fudge into 36 squares with knife. Refrigerate until firm. Cut into squares. Wrap in plastic wrap and top with bows as shown in photo on page 65.

Makes 36 pieces

Coconut Snowball Cocoa

For coconut lovers only! A triple dose of this tropical treat plus a floating ice cream snowball makes ordinary hot chocolate extraordinary.

- 1 **pint vanilla ice cream**
- 1 **cup flaked coconut**
- ½ **cup unsweetened cocoa**
- 1 **quart milk**
- ½ **cup dark rum (optional)**
- ¾ **to 1 cup cream of coconut**
- 1 **teaspoon coconut extract**
- ½ **cup chocolate-flavored ice cream sauce (optional)**
- 8 **maraschino cherries (optional)**

1. Scoop ice cream into 8 small balls; immediately roll in coconut. Place on waxed paper-lined baking sheet; freeze until ready to use.

2. Whisk cocoa into milk in large saucepan. Stir in rum, if desired, cream of coconut and coconut extract. Bring to a simmer over medium-high heat. Pour into 8 large heatproof mugs.

3. Float ice cream balls in cocoa. If desired, drizzle each ice cream ball with chocolate sauce and top with a cherry.

Makes 8 servings
(about 6 ounces each)

Banana Nog

Banana adds a surprisingly delicious flavor and creaminess to eggnog. Festive candy cane stirrers make serving it even more fun!

INGREDIENTS

- **2 cups milk**
- **1 large ripe banana, cut into pieces**
- **½ cup sugar**
- **1 tablespoon cornstarch**
- **2 egg yolks***
- **⅔ cup light rum**
- **¼ cup crème de cacao**
- **1 teaspoon vanilla**
- **2 cups half-and-half, chilled**
- **Whipped cream**
- **Unsweetened cocoa**
- **6 miniature candy canes**

SUPPLIES

Red and/or green ribbon

1. Process milk and banana in blender or food processor until smooth. Mix sugar and cornstarch in medium saucepan; stir in milk mixture. Heat to simmering over medium heat, stirring occasionally.

2. Lightly beat egg yolks in small bowl; whisk about ½ cup milk mixture into egg yolks.

Whisk yolk mixture back into saucepan. Cook over medium heat, stirring constantly, until thick enough to coat the back of a spoon. *Do not boil.*

3. Remove from heat; stir in rum, liqueur and vanilla. Pour into large heatproof pitcher or bowl. Cover; refrigerate until chilled.

4. Just before serving, stir half-and-half into eggnog mixture. Serve in mugs or punch cups; garnish with dollops of whipped cream and a sprinkle of cocoa. Tie pieces of ribbon around candy canes; use as stirrers.

Makes 6 servings
(about 6 ounces each)

*Use only grade A clean, uncracked eggs.

Poinsettia Pie

A stunning poinsettia made from chocolate leaves adorns this refreshing mint-flavored pie.

2 cups chocolate wafer crumbs
6 tablespoons butter or margarine, melted
⅛ teaspoon peppermint extract (optional)
¾ cup sugar, divided
1 envelope unflavored gelatin
⅓ cup cold water
3 eggs, separated*
⅓ cup crème de menthe
½ cup whipping cream, whipped
Chocolate Leaves (recipe follows)
1 round yellow candy

* Use only grade A clean, uncracked eggs.

1. Preheat oven to 350°F. Combine cookie crumbs, butter and peppermint extract, if desired, in small bowl. Press onto bottom and up side of 9-inch pie plate. Bake 8 minutes. Cool on wire rack.

2. Combine ½ cup sugar and gelatin in small saucepan. Add cold water; let stand 1 minute. Stir over low heat until gelatin is completely dissolved.

3. Beat egg yolks in small bowl. Stir about ¼ cup gelatin mixture into egg yolks; return egg yolk mixture to saucepan. Cook over low heat, stirring constantly, until thick enough to coat the back of a spoon. Remove from heat; stir in liqueur. Cool to room temperature.

4. Beat egg whites until foamy. Gradually beat in remaining ¼ cup sugar; continue beating until soft peaks form. Fold into gelatin mixture. Gently fold in whipped cream. Pour into cooled crust. Refrigerate until firm, 8 hours or overnight.

5. Prepare Chocolate Leaves, reserving small amount of melted chocolate.

6. Arrange Chocolate Leaves on pie as shown in photo to create poinsettia, using reserved chocolate to attach. Place yellow candy in center as shown. Refrigerate until serving time.

Makes 1 (9-inch) pie

Chocolate Leaves

INGREDIENTS
¾ cup coarsely chopped white chocolate baking bars or confectionery coating
Shortening
Red food color
¾ cup coarsely chopped semisweet chocolate

SUPPLIES
Pastry brush
6 to 8 medium and 4 or 5 large lemon leaves**

**These non-toxic leaves are available in florist shops.

Clockwise from top left: *Banana Nog (page 67); Coconut Snowball Cocoa (page 66); Poinsettia Pie*

1. Melt white chocolate in top of double boiler over hot, not boiling water, stirring constantly. Stir in red food color, a few drops at a time, until desired color is reached. If chocolate begins to thicken or loses its shine, stir in shortening, 1 teaspoon at a time.

2. Brush thin layer of pink chocolate on back side of each medium-sized leaf with pastry brush. Do not spread to edge of leaf. Place on waxed paper-lined baking sheet. Refrigerate about 30 minutes or until firm.

3. Repeat with semisweet chocolate and large leaves. Refrigerate about 30 minutes or until firm.

4. Gently peel chocolate off leaves, beginning at stem ends. Refrigerate until ready to use.
Makes about 12 leaves

Sweet Leaf Wreath

This wreath of cookie and chocolate leaves makes a pretty centerpiece encircling a candle.

INGREDIENTS

**Chocolate Leaves
(page 68)
1 recipe Gingerbread
Cookie dough (page 92)
1 egg white*
1 cup confectioners' sugar
Red cinnamon candies**

SUPPLIES

**1 (8-inch) cardboard circle
Red ribbon bow**

1. Prepare Chocolate Leaves using semisweet chocolate only; set aside.

2. Preheat oven to 350°F. Grease cookie sheets.

3. Roll dough on floured surface to ⅛-inch thickness. Using diagrams as guides, cut out 8 holly leaves and 8 rounded leaves (see Making Patterns, page 3). Mark veins in leaves with tip of knife as shown in photo.

4. Bake 8 to 10 minutes until edges begin to brown. Remove to wire racks; cool completely.

5. Cut center out of cardboard circle leaving a 2-inch-wide ring. Cover ring with foil. Arrange cookies as shown in photo on cardboard ring.

6. Combine egg white and confectioners' sugar in small bowl; beat well. Use frosting to attach leaves to cardboard ring and to each other.**

7. Decorate with red cinnamon candies, Chocolate Leaves and bow as shown, attaching with frosting.   *Makes 1 wreath*

*Use only grade A clean, uncracked eggs.

**To prevent frosting from drying, keep bowl of frosting covered with damp towel while working.

Note: *This wreath is designed to be a centerpiece. It may not be sturdy enough to hang.*

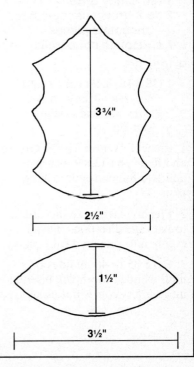

Sweet Leaf Wreath

Jolly Ole Saint Nick Cake

Perfect for someone celebrating a Christmas birthday or for any special gathering during the holiday season.

INGREDIENTS

2 packages (18.25 ounces *each*) yellow cake mix, plus ingredients to prepare mixes
3 containers (16 ounces *each*) vanilla frosting
2 tablespoons milk
Red food color
Chocolate sprinkles
2 black licorice drops
1 black licorice whip
1 red candy drop
2 dark brown candy-coated chocolate pieces
7 chocolate nonpareils

SUPPLIES

1 (18 × 18-inch) cake board, covered, or large tray
Pastry bag and medium star tip

1. Preheat oven to 350°F. Grease and flour one 13 × 9-inch pan and two 8-inch round baking pans.

2. Prepare cake mixes according to package directions. Divide evenly into prepared cake pans.

3. Bake 35 to 40 minutes or until wooden toothpick inserted into centers comes out clean.

Cool in pans on wire racks 10 minutes; remove from pans and cool completely.

4. Using diagrams 1 and 2 as guide, cut out pieces (see Making Patterns, page 3).

5. Combine 1 container frosting and milk. Position pieces on prepared cake board as shown in diagram 3, connecting with some of the thinned frosting. Frost entire cake with remaining thinned frosting.

6. Frost face area with some of the white frosting. Reserve remaining white frosting for piping.

7. Color remaining container frosting with red food color. Frost hat, shirt and pants with the red frosting, reserving small portion for piping.

8. Using star tip and red frosting, pipe design on hat. Using star tip and reserved white frosting, pipe beard, cuffs and trim of hat. Decorate with candies as shown in photo.

Makes 14 to 16 servings

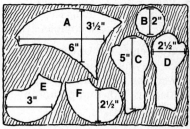

1

Jolly Ole Saint Nick Cake

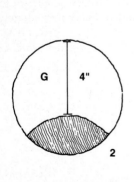

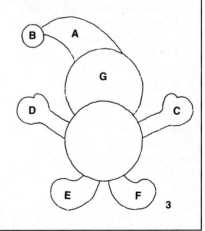

Christmas Castle

You can almost imagine Santa and his elves residing in this fairyland castle. It's magically easy to make—no baking needed!

INGREDIENTS

2 containers (16 ounces *each*) vanilla frosting
**1 ice cream sugar cone
Decorations: Nonpareils, candy canes, chocolate-covered wafer cookies, red cinnamon candies, red and green gumdrops, miniature butter cookies, miniature fudge-striped cookies, candy fruit slices and other assorted cookies and candies**
1 Festive Popcorn Treat (page 53), optional

SUPPLIES

1 empty ½-gallon milk or juice carton, rinsed and dried
1 empty 1-quart milk or juice carton, rinsed and cleaned
1 empty ½-pint cream carton, rinsed and dried
1 (13 × 11-inch) cake board, covered, or large tray

1. Fold down pointed ends of milk cartons to make flat surface; tape securely. Tape cream carton closed at top; tape to top of 1-quart carton. Cover with foil. Tape securely to cake board.

2. Spread castle with frosting. Place ice cream cone on top of ½ gallon carton; frost. Decorate with cookies and candies as shown in photo. Position popcorn tree near castle, if desired.   *Makes 1 castle*

Note: Surround castle with shredded coconut to look like freshly fallen snow.

Cranberry Snow Punch

Scoops of frozen yogurt resemble melting snowballs in this refreshing seasonal punch.

1 cup apple juice, chilled
½ cup superfine sugar
1½ cups cranberry juice cocktail, chilled
1½ cups bitter lemon or tonic water, chilled
1 pint vanilla frozen yogurt

1. Combine apple juice and sugar in punch bowl; stir until sugar dissolves. Stir in cranberry juice and bitter lemon.

2. Scoop frozen yogurt onto top of punch. Serve immediately.
Makes 8 servings (about 4 ounces each)

Christmas Castle

Kittens and Mittens

Kittens and Mittens

These charming strings of cookies will bring Christmas cheer to a tree or mantle.

INGREDIENTS

1 recipe Chocolate Cookie Dough (page 92)
1 recipe Cookie Glaze (page 93)
Assorted food colors
Assorted candies

SUPPLIES

Plastic drinking straw
Reclosable plastic sandwich bags for piping
Yarn or ribbon

1. Preheat oven to 325°F. Grease cookie sheets.

2. Roll dough on floured surface to ⅛-inch thickness. Using diagrams 1 and 2 as guides, cut out kitten and mitten cookies (see Making Patterns page 3). Place cookies on prepared cookie sheets. With plastic straw, make holes in tops of cookies, about ½ inch from top edges.

3. Bake 8 to 10 minutes until edges begin to brown. Remove to wire racks; cool completely. If necessary, push straw through warm cookies to remake holes.

4. Place cookies on racks on waxed paper-lined baking sheets. Spoon Cookie Glaze into several small bowls. Color as desired with food color. Spoon glaze over cookies. Place some of remaining glaze in plastic bag. Cut tiny tip from corner of bag. Use to pipe decorations as shown in photo. Decorate with candies as shown. Let stand until glaze has set.

4. Thread yarn or ribbon through holes to make garland.

Makes about 2 dozen cookies

Hot Mulled Cider

A fragrant punch created to warm you up on a chilly winter night.

½ gallon apple cider
½ cup packed light brown sugar
1½ teaspoons balsamic or cider vinegar
1 teaspoon vanilla
1 cinnamon stick
6 whole cloves
½ cup applejack or bourbon (optional)

Combine all ingredients except applejack in large saucepan; bring to a boil. Reduce heat to low; simmer, uncovered, 10 minutes. Remove from heat; stir in applejack. Pour into punch bowl. *Makes 16 servings (about 4 ounces each)*

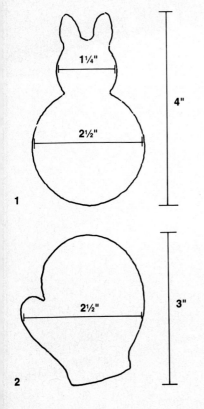

WINTER FUN

Hanukkah Honey Cake

A beautiful menorah tops this delicious honey spice cake.

INGREDIENTS

3 eggs
¾ cup packed brown sugar
¾ cup vegetable oil
1¼ cups honey
⅔ cup strong coffee
3 cups all-purpose flour
1½ teaspoons baking powder
1 teaspoon baking soda
½ teaspoon ground allspice
½ teaspoon ground cinnamon
½ teaspoon ground nutmeg
¾ cup chopped walnuts
1½ teaspoons grated orange peel
1 teaspoon grated lemon peel
2 containers (16 ounces *each*) vanilla frosting
Yellow food color

SUPPLIES

1 (13×9-inch) cake board, covered, or large tray
Pastry bag and medium writing and star tips
8 small white candles

1. Preheat oven to 325°F. Grease and flour 13×9-inch baking pan.

2. Beat eggs in large bowl at high speed of electric mixer until thick and lemon colored, about 5 minutes. Beat in brown sugar and oil. Add honey and coffee;

Hanukkah Honey Cake

stir well. Combine flour, baking powder, baking soda and spices in small bowl; add to batter and stir well. Stir in walnuts and grated peels. Pour into pan.

3. Bake 40 to 45 minutes until cake is golden and wooden toothpick inserted into center comes out clean. Cool in pan on wire rack 15 minutes. Remove from pan to rack; cool.

4. Place cake on prepared cake board. Frost top and sides of cake with 1 container frosting.

5. Using diagram as guide, cut pattern (see Making Patterns, page 3). Position pattern on cake as shown in photo. Trace around pattern with wooden toothpick; remove pattern.

6. Color remaining container frosting yellow. Spoon frosting into pastry bag fitted with medium writing tip. Outline menorah pattern with frosting. Using star tip, fill in menorah and pipe decorative border around edge of cake. Insert candles.

Makes 12 to 14 servings

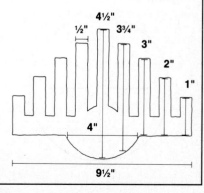

Snowflake Breads

Just like real snowflakes, no two of these pretty breads are the same.

> **1 package (16 ounces)
>   hot roll mix, plus
>   ingredients to prepare
>   mix**
> **¼ cup grated Parmesan
>   cheese**
> **1 teaspoon dried basil
>   leaves**
> **1 egg yolk**
> **1 teaspoon water
>   Coarse salt, optional**

1. Prepare hot roll mix according to package directions adding Parmesan and basil. Knead dough on lightly floured surface until smooth, about 5 minutes. Cover loosely; let stand in bowl about 15 minutes.

2. Preheat oven to 400°F. Grease cookie sheets.

3. Divide dough into 12 equal pieces. Pat each piece into 2- to 3-inch circle. Place on prepared cookie sheet. With scissors, snip 8 slits in each circle as shown in diagram.

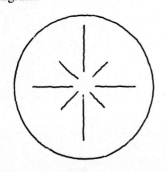

4. Carefully stretch dough to open slits and form snowflake shape. Cover loosely; let rise until doubled in size about 30 minutes.

5. Combine egg yolk and water. Lightly brush tops of breads; sprinkle with coarse salt, if desired. Bake about 15 minutes or until golden. Serve warm.

Makes 12 breads

Snowman Cupcakes

The perfect treat for a winter birthday or after a fun day playing in the snow.

INGREDIENTS

> **1 package (18.5 ounces)
>   yellow or white cake
>   mix, plus ingredients to
>   prepare mix**
> **2 containers (16 ounces
>   *each*) vanilla frosting**
> **4 cups flaked coconut**
> **15 large marshmallows**
> **15 miniature chocolate
>   covered peanut butter
>   cups, unwrapped**
> **Decorations: Small red
>   candies and pretzel
>   sticks**
> **Green and red decorating
>   gel**

SUPPLIES

> **15 (2½-inch) paper baking cups**
> **15 (1-inch) paper baking cups**

Snowman Cupcakes

1. Preheat oven to 350°F. Line 15 regular-size (2½-inch) muffin pan cups and 15 small (about 1 inch) muffin pan cups with paper muffin cups.

2. Prepare cake mix according to package directions. Spoon batter into prepared muffin pans.

3. Bake 10 to 15 minutes for small cupcakes and 15 to 20 minutes for large cupcakes or until cupcakes are golden and wooden toothpick inserted into centers comes out clean. Cool in pans on wire rack 10 minutes. Remove to racks; cool completely. Remove paper liners.

4. For each snowman, frost bottom and side of 1 large cupcake; coat with coconut. Repeat with 1 small cupcake. Attach small cupcake to large cupcake with some frosting. Attach marshmallow to small cupcake with frosting.

5. Attach inverted peanut butter cup to marshmallow with frosting. Use pretzels for arms and small red candies for buttons as shown in photo. Pipe faces with decorating gel as shown. Repeat with remaining cupcakes. *Makes 15 snowmen*

Confetti New Year's Resolution Cookies; Minutes to Midnight Cake

Confetti New Year's Resolution Cookies

These colorful cookies hold ready-made resolutions to help you ring in the new year.

INGREDIENTS
- ⅓ cup all-purpose flour
- 6 tablespoons sugar
- 1 tablespoon cornstarch
- ⅛ teaspoon salt
- ⅓ cup water
- ¼ cup vegetable oil
- 1 egg white
- 1 teaspoon vanilla
- Assorted food colors

SUPPLIES
Prepared resolutions (see Note)

1. Combine flour, sugar, cornstarch and salt in small bowl. Add water, oil, egg white and vanilla; stir until smooth. Divide into 3 bowls. Use 1 or 2 drops food color to color batter in each bowl.

2. Grease small skillet. Heat over medium heat. Spoon 1 tablespoon batter into pan, spreading to 3-inch circle with back of spoon. Cook 5 minutes or until golden brown on bottom. Turn over; cook 1 minute.

3. Remove cookie from skillet and place, darker side up, on flat surface. Immediately place prepared resolution in center of cookie. Fold cookie in half as shown in diagram 1. Fold over edge of bowl as shown in diagram 2.

4. Place in muffin pan to hold shape while cooling. Repeat with remaining batter.

Makes 3 dozen cookies

Note: Type resolutions (or write them in pencil, not ink) on 2 × ½-inch pieces of paper. Be sure to have all your resolutions prepared ahead of time because you must work quickly once you start making the cookies. Here are some ideas to get you started:

• *I will smile more*
• *Reduce, reuse, recycle*
• *I resolve to be kinder to fellow humans*
• *Live long and prosper*
• *I will make my first million before I'm 30 (40?, 50?)*

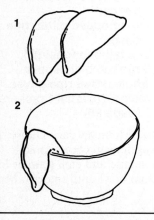

Minutes to Midnight Cake

Quick! Before the clock strikes 12 have one more piece of this dense, fudgy "to-die-for" cake.

INGREDIENTS

12 ounces semisweet chocolate, coarsely chopped, divided
2 squares (1 ounce *each*) unsweetened chocolate, coarsely chopped
1 cup plus 1 tablespoon butter or margarine, divided
5 eggs
¼ cup sugar
⅓ cup light corn syrup
½ teaspoon vanilla
1⅓ cups whipping cream, divided
3 white chocolate baking bars (2 ounces *each*), coarsely chopped, divided

SUPPLIES
Pastry bag and large star tip

1. Preheat oven to 325°F. Grease and flour 9-inch springform pan.

2. Melt 6 ounces semisweet chocolate, unsweetened chocolate and 1 cup butter over low heat in medium saucepan, stirring constantly; cool slightly. Beat eggs and sugar in large bowl. Add corn syrup and vanilla; beat well. Stir in

continued

Minutes to Midnight Cake *continued*
chocolate mixture. Pour batter into prepared pan.

3. Bake 45 to 55 minutes or until wooden toothpick inserted in center of cake comes out clean. Cool completely in pan on wire rack. Remove side of pan.

4. Bring ⅔ cup cream and remaining 1 tablespoon butter to a simmer in small saucepan over low heat; remove from heat. Add remaining 6 ounces semisweet chocolate, stirring until completely melted. Pour into bowl; cover and refrigerate until mixture thickens but is still pourable, about 1½ hours.

5. Place cake on wire rack over waxed paper-lined baking sheet. Pour chocolate mixture over cake; spread to cover top and sides. Refrigerate until chilled, about 2 hours.

6. Draw numbers, dots and clock hands as shown in photo on page 82 on piece of paper. Place paper on cookie sheet. Cover with sheet of waxed paper; tape waxed paper to cookie sheet. Melt 2 ounces of white chocolate; pipe white chocolate onto waxed paper following drawings (see Piping Chocolate, page 5). Refrigerate until firm.

7. Bring remaining ⅔ cup cream to a simmer in small saucepan over medium heat; remove from heat. Add remaining 4 ounces white chocolate, stirring until completely melted. Refrigerate until chilled, about 30 minutes.

8. Beat chilled cream mixture just until soft peaks form. Using pastry bag and large star tip, pipe along top and bottom edges of cake as shown.

9. Carefully peel numbers and clock hands from waxed paper; place on cake as shown. Refrigerate until ready to serve.
Makes 10 servings

New Year's Crystal Ball

Look into this heavenly crystal ball and see a great-tasting future!

10 ounces (2½ cups) shredded Monterey Jack cheese
2 packages (3 ounces *each*) cream cheese, softened, divided
⅓ cup finely chopped onion
¼ cup mayonnaise
1 teaspoon chili powder
⅓ cup chopped red bell pepper
⅓ cup chopped pitted ripe olives
1 to 2 tablespoons milk
1 large red bell pepper
6 whole pitted ripe olives
1 recipe Celestial Crackers (page 85)

1. Beat Monterey Jack cheese, 1 package cream cheese, onion, mayonnaise and chili powder in medium bowl until smooth. Mix

New Year's Crystal Ball with Celestial Crackers

in chopped red pepper and chopped olives. Shape mixture into ball. Cover with plastic wrap and refrigerate until firm, about 2 hours.

2. Beat remaining package cream cheese in small bowl until fluffy; beat in enough milk to make good spreading consistency. Spread mixture on cheese ball; refrigerate loosely covered until serving time.

3. Cut red pepper into stars with small cutter or sharp knife. Slice olives into crescent moons.

4. Just before serving, decorate cheese ball with stars and moons. Place cheese ball on inverted mug or small plate. Serve with Celestial Crackers.

Makes 12 to 14 servings

Celestial Crackers

These tasty homemade crackers are the perfect accompaniment to the New Year's Crystal Ball.

INGREDIENTS
  1 cup all-purpose flour
  ½ teaspoon baking powder
  ½ teaspoon paprika
  ¼ teaspoon salt
  ⅓ cup plus 1 tablespoon
      water, divided
  3 tablespoons vegetable oil
  1 egg white
      Toppings: Sesame seeds,
      poppy seeds, garlic salt
      and dried herbs

SUPPLIES
  2-inch star- and moon-
      shaped cookie cutters

continued

85

Celestial Crackers *continued*

1. Combine flour, baking powder, paprika and salt in medium bowl. Stir in ⅓ cup water and oil to form smooth dough.

2. Preheat oven to 400°F. Grease baking sheets.

3. Roll dough on floured surface to 14×12-inch rectangle. Cut dough into star and moon shapes using cutters. Place on prepared baking sheets.

4. Combine egg white and 1 tablespoon water; brush on crackers. Sprinkle with toppings.

5. Bake 8 to 10 minutes until edges begin to brown. Remove to wire rack; cool completely.

Makes 2½ dozen

Decadent Truffle Tree

Nobody can resist this beautiful centerpiece made of creamy, decadent truffles.

INGREDIENTS

1⅓ cups whipping cream
¼ cup packed brown sugar
¼ teaspoon salt
¼ cup light rum
2 teaspoons vanilla
16 ounces semisweet chocolate, chopped
16 ounces milk chocolate, chopped
Finely chopped nuts and assorted sprinkles

Decadent Truffle Tree

SUPPLIES

1 (9-inch tall) foam cone
About 70 wooden toothpicks

1. Heat cream, sugar, salt, rum and vanilla in medium saucepan over medium heat until sugar is dissolved and mixture is hot. Remove from heat; add chocolates, stirring until melted, (return pan to low heat if necessary). Pour into shallow dish. Cover and refrigerate until just firm, about 1 hour.

2. Shape about half the mixture into 1¼-inch balls. Shape remaining mixture into ¾-inch balls. Roll balls in nuts and sprinkles. Refrigerate truffles until firm, about 1 hour.

3. Cover cone with foil. Starting at bottom of cone, attach larger truffles with wooden toothpicks. Use smaller truffles toward the top of the cone. Refrigerate until serving time.

Makes 1 tree (6 dozen truffles)

Note: *If kitchen is very warm, keep portion of truffle mixture chilled as you shape and roll balls.*

Hanukkah Fried Cruller Bows

A traditional Hanukkah treat, these delightful bows are wonderful served warm with a sprinkle of cinnamon and sugar.

INGREDIENTS

1¼ cups all-purpose flour
3 tablespoons confectioners' sugar
2 tablespoons granulated sugar
½ teaspoon salt
1 whole egg
2 egg whites
1 teaspoon vanilla
Vegetable oil, for frying
Confectioners' sugar
Ground cinnamon

SUPPLIES

Deep-frying thermometer

1. Combine flour, 3 tablespoons confectioners' sugar, granulated sugar and salt in small bowl. Stir in whole egg, egg whites and vanilla with fork until mixture is crumbly.

2. Form dough into ball; knead on lightly floured surface until smooth, about 5 minutes. Cover loosely; let stand about 30 minutes.

3. Heat 2 inches oil to 375°F in heavy, large saucepan. Roll dough on floured surface to 12×12-inch square, about ⅛ inch thick. Cut into 12 (1-inch) strips; cut strips in half to form 24 (6×1-inch) strips. Tie each strip into a knot.

4. Fry knots in oil, a few at a time, 3 to 4 minutes or until golden. Drain on paper towels. Sprinkle with confectioners' sugar and cinnamon. Serve warm.   *Makes 2 dozen bows*

Raspberry Wine Punch

This delicious punch is served in a decorated ice block. It looks beautiful on the table and keeps the punch cold all party long.

INGREDIENTS

1 package (10 ounces) frozen red raspberries in syrup, thawed
1 bottle (750 mL) white zinfandel or blush wine
¼ cup raspberry-flavored liqueur
3 to 4 cups distilled* water, divided
Fresh cranberries

SUPPLIES

Empty ½ gallon milk or juice carton
Sprigs of pine and tinsel
Funnel

Distilled water helps makes a crystal-clear ice mold.

1. Process raspberries in food processor or blender until smooth; press through strainer, discarding seeds. Combine wine, raspberry purée and liqueur in pitcher; refrigerate until serving time. Rinse out wine bottle and remove label.

2. Fully open top of carton. Place wine bottle in center of carton. Tape bottle securely to carton so bottle will not move when adding water. Pour 2 cups distilled water into carton. Carefully push pine sprigs, cranberries and tinsel into water between bottle and carton to form decorative design. Add remaining water to almost fill carton. Freeze until firm, 8 hours or overnight.

3. Just before serving, peel carton from ice block. Using funnel, pour punch back into wine bottle. Wrap bottom of ice block with white cotton napkin or towel to hold while serving.

*Makes 8 servings
(about 4 ounces each)*

Note: *Punch may also be served in a punch bowl if desired.*

Raspberry Wine Punch

Football Calzones

To make these tasty gridiron treats extra easy, make the filling mixture ahead of time and shape, fill and bake when you are ready to serve.

1 package (16 ounces) hot roll mix, plus ingredients to prepare mix
1 pound hot or mild Italian sausage, casing removed, crumbled
1½ cups chopped broccoli
¼ cup chopped roasted red peppers* or pimiento
1 clove garlic, minced
8 ounces (2 cups) shredded mozzarella cheese
Olive or vegetable oil

*Look for roasted red peppers packed in cans or jars in the Italian food section of the supermarket.

1. Prepare hot roll mix according to package directions. Knead dough on lightly floured surface until smooth, about 5 minutes. Cover loosely; let stand in bowl about 15 minutes.

2. Cook sausage in large skillet over medium-high heat until browned. Drain on paper towels; discard all but 1 teaspoon drippings. Add broccoli to skillet; cook over medium heat 5 minutes. Add peppers and garlic; cook about 5 minutes or until broccoli is crisp-tender. Remove from heat. Stir in drained sausage and cheese.

3. Preheat oven to 375°F. Grease baking sheets.

4. Roll dough on floured surface to ¼-inch thickness. Cut into 16 football shapes as shown in diagram 1. Combine scraps and reroll dough if necessary. Place 8 football shapes on prepared baking sheets. Spoon about ⅓ cup sausage mixture on shapes on baking sheets. Top with remaining shapes; press edges with fork to seal. Using dough scraps, decorate to resemble football as shown in diagram 2.

5. Brush tops of footballs with oil. Cover loosely; let rise in warm place until doubled in size, about 30 minutes.

6. Bake 20 to 25 minutes or until golden. Refrigerate leftovers.   *Makes 8 calzones*

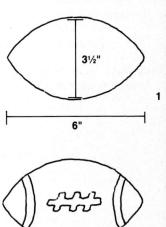

3½"

6"

1

2

New Year's Toast Dip

Toast in the new year with this tasty dip served in a champagne glass.

**2 packages (3 ounces *each*)
   cream cheese, softened**
½ cup half-and-half or milk
⅓ cup mayonnaise
⅔ cup chopped crabmeat
**2 tablespoons chopped
   green onion**
**2 teaspoons ranch dressing
   mix (dry)**
**Sliced green olives
   (optional)**
**Assorted fresh
   vegetables**

1. Beat cream cheese in small bowl at medium speed of electric mixer until fluffy; beat in half-and-half and mayonnaise. Stir in crabmeat, onion and salad dressing mix. Refrigerate 1 hour or until serving time.

2. Spoon dip into champagne glass or other glass or goblet with wide opening; garnish with olive slices. Serve with assorted fresh vegetables.

Makes about 2 cups dip

Pineapple-Champagne Punch

Every New Year's party needs a champagne punch, but this one gets a real "punch" from pineapple.

1 quart pineapple sherbet
**1 quart unsweetened
   pineapple juice, chilled**
**1 bottle (750 mL) dry
   champagne, chilled**
**2 fresh or canned pineapple
   slices, each slice cut
   into 6 wedges**
Mint sprigs

1. Process sherbet and pineapple juice in blender until smooth and frothy. Pour into punch bowl. Stir in champagne.

2. Float pineapple wedges in punch in groups of 3 or 4 to form flowers; garnish with mint sprigs. Serve immediately.

*Makes 20 servings
(about 4 ounces each)*

BASIC RECIPES

Note: Yield, preparation and baking times may vary for cookies. For best results, prepare and bake as directed in individual recipes.

Chocolate Cookies

1 cup butter or margarine, softened
1 cup sugar
1 egg
1 teaspoon vanilla
2 ounces semisweet chocolate, melted
2¼ cups all-purpose flour
1 teaspoon baking powder
¼ teaspoon salt

1. Beat butter and sugar in large bowl at high speed of electric mixer until fluffy. Beat in egg and vanilla. Add melted chocolate; mix well. Add flour, baking powder and salt; mix well. Cover; refrigerate until firm, about 2 hours.

2. Preheat oven to 325°F. Grease cookie sheets.

3. Roll dough on floured surface to ⅛-inch thickness. Cut into desired shapes with cookie cutters. Place on prepared cookie sheets.

4. Bake 8 to 10 minutes or until set. Remove to wire racks; cool completely.
   Makes about 3 dozen cookies

Gingerbread Cookies

½ cup shortening
⅓ cup packed light brown sugar
¼ cup dark molasses
1 egg white
½ teaspoon vanilla
1½ cups all-purpose flour
½ teaspoon baking soda
¼ teaspoon baking powder
½ teaspoon salt
1 teaspoon ground cinnamon
½ teaspoon ground ginger

1. Beat shortening, brown sugar, molasses, egg white and vanilla in large bowl at high speed of electric mixer until smooth. Combine flour, baking soda, baking powder, salt and spices in small bowl. Add to shortening mixture; mix well. Cover; refrigerate until firm, about 8 hours or overnight.

2. Preheat oven to 350°F. Grease cookie sheets.

3. Roll dough on floured surface to ⅛-inch thickness. Cut into desired shapes with cookie cutters. Place on prepared cookie sheets.

4. Bake 6 to 8 minutes or until edges begin to brown. Remove to wire racks; cool completely.
   Makes about 2½ dozen cookies

Butter Cookies

¾ cup butter or margarine,
softened
¼ cup granulated sugar
¼ cup packed light brown
sugar
1 egg yolk
1¾ cups all-purpose flour
¾ teaspoon baking powder
⅛ teaspoon salt

1. Combine butter, granulated sugar, brown sugar and egg yolk in medium bowl. Add flour, baking powder and salt; mix well. Cover; refrigerate until firm, about 4 hours or overnight.

2. Preheat oven to 350°F.

3. Roll dough on floured surface to ¼-inch thickness. Cut into desired shapes with cookie cutters. Place on ungreased cookie sheets.

4. Bake 8 to 10 minutes or until edges begin to brown. Remove to wire racks; cool completely.

Makes about 2 dozen cookies

Fluffy White Frosting

1 container (16 ounces)
vanilla frosting
¾ cup marshmallow creme

Combine frosting and marshmallow creme in medium bowl; mix well.

Makes about 2 cups

Marzipan

1 can (8 ounces) almond
paste
1 egg white*
3 cups confectioners' sugar

1. Combine almond paste and egg white in small bowl. Add 2 cups confectioners' sugar; mix well.** Knead in remaining 1 cup sugar until smooth and pliable.

2. Wrap tightly in plastic wrap; refrigerate until ready to use.

Makes about 2 cups

*Use only grade A clean, uncracked eggs.

**If coloring marzipan, stir in desired amount of food color before kneading in remaining 1 cup confectioners' sugar.

Cookie Glaze

4 cups confectioners' sugar
4 to 6 tablespoons milk
Assorted food color

1. Combine confectioners' sugar and enough milk to make a medium-thick pourable glaze.

2. Color as desired with food color.

3. Place cookies on wire rack on waxed paper-lined baking sheet. Spoon glaze over cookies; allow to dry completely.

Makes about 4 cups glaze

Index

METRIC CONVERSION CHART

VOLUME MEASUREMENTS (dry)

⅛ teaspoon = 0.5 mL

¼ teaspoon = 1 mL

½ teaspoon = 2 mL

¾ teaspoon = 4 mL

1 teaspoon = 5 mL

1 tablespoon = 15 mL

2 tablespoons = 30 mL

¼ cup = 60 mL

⅓ cup = 75 mL

½ cup = 125 mL

⅔ cup = 150 mL

¼ cup = 175 mL

1 cup = 250 mL

2 cups = 1 pint = 500 mL

3 cups = 750 mL

4 cups = 1 quart = 1 L

VOLUME MEASUREMENTS (fluid)

1 fluid ounce (2 tablespoons) = 30 mL

4 fluid ounces (½ cup) = 125 mL

8 fluid ounces (1 cup) = 250 mL

12 fluid ounces (1½ cups) = 375 mL

16 fluid ounces (2 cups) = 500 mL

WEIGHTS (mass)

½ ounce = 15 g

1 ounce = 30 g

3 ounces = 90 g

4 ounces = 120 g

8 ounces = 225 g

10 ounces = 285 g

12 ounces = 360 g

16 ounces = 1 pound = 450 g

DIMENSIONS

1/16 inch = 2 mm

⅛ inch = 3 mm

¼ inch = 6 mm

½ inch = 1.5 cm

¾ inch = 2 cm

1 inch = 2.5 cm

OVEN TEMPERATURES

250°F = 120°C

275°F = 140°C

300°F = 150°C

325°F = 160°C

350°F = 180°C

375°F = 190°C

400°F = 200°C

425°F = 220°C

450°F = 230°C

BAKING PAN SIZES

Utensil	Size in Inches/Quarts	Metric Volume	Size in Centimeters
Baking or Cake Pan (square or rectangular)	8 × 8 × 2	2 L	20 × 20 × 5
	9 × 9 × 2	2.5 L	22 × 22 × 5
	12 × 8 × 2	3 L	30 × 20 × 5
	13 × 9 × 2	3.5 L	33 × 23 × 5
Loaf Pan	8 × 4 × 3	1.5 L	20 × 10 × 7
	9 × 5 × 3	2 L	23 × 13 × 7
Round Layer Cake Pan	8 × 1½	1.2 L	20 × 4
	9 × 1½	1.5 L	23 × 4
Pie Plate	8 × 1¼	750 mL	20 × 3
	9 × 1¼	1 L	23 × 3
Baking Dish or Casserole	1 quart	1 L	—
	1½ quart	1.5 L	—
	2 quart	2 L	—